Praise for *The Give-Back Solution*

"In today's society, creating accessible opportunities to reach out across global boundaries is more important than ever. *The Give-Back Solution* navigates you through a diverse array of unique opportunities with practical advice and genuine stories from the field for many types of volunteers and interests. This is an invaluable resource for anyone interested in giving back in a global-2.0 way."
—Steve Rosenthal, chairperson, Building Bridges Coalition, and executive director and founder, Cross-Cultural Solutions

"Susan Skog brings to light a modern insurgency of the most noble kind. *The Give-Back Solution* chronicles a growing movement of everyday folks who are choosing to travel thousands of miles to contribute their time, energy, and compassion in effort to help make a better world, and along the way, finding hope in the planet's bleakest places and discovering shared human values in places poles apart. Skog's examples of the kind of transformations that can occur, for both the volunteers and the communities they serve, will buoy the spirits of even the greatest cynics and inspire a new generation of traveling humanitarians."
—Natasha Carvell, director of Travel for Good, Travelocity

"We're living in a time when everyone's called to be of service, to lift up a bit of our interconnected world with our gifts. And through the stories of everyday volunteers, this book magnificently shows that helping others is the best medicine there is. We think a lot less about our own troubles when we're serving someone else. Susan Skog has shown us that giving back ultimately gives us the warm connections, happiness and health we all seek."

—Joan Borysenko, author of *Your Soul's Compass* and *Inner Peace for Busy People*

THE
GIVE-BACK
SOLUTION

Create a Better World
with Your
TIME, TALENTS, AND TRAVEL
(WHETHER YOU HAVE $10 or $10,000)

SUSAN SKOG

SOURCEBOOKS, INC.®
NAPERVILLE, ILLINOIS

Published by Sourcebooks, Inc.
P.O. Box 4410, Naperville, Illinois 60567–4410
(630) 961–3900
Fax: (630) 961–2168
www.sourcebooks.com

Library of Congress Cataloging-in-Publication Data

Skog, Susan
  The give-back solution : create a better world with your time, talents, and travel (whether you have $10 or $10,000) / Susan Skog.
      p. cm.
  1. Voluntarism. 2. Volunteers. 3. Humanitarian assistance. 4. Social action. 5. Helping behavior. I. Title.
  HN49.V64S59 2009
  361.2'6--dc22
                                    2008038835

Printed and bound in the United States of America.
VP 10 9 8 7 6 5 4 3 2 1

Dedication

To my parents Bob and Vivian Stuekerjuergen and
my father- and mother-in-law Clarence and Jean Skog,
who've shown me for years what it means
to roll up your sleeves and give back.

Contents

Acknowledgments

First, I have to recognize my agent, Lindsay Edgecombe. I am grateful that all the literary roads led to you and Levine Greenberg. Your wise guidance and strategic vision for this book helped it find its publishing home. Your kindness and personal resonance with my message helped me bring it home late at night! I'm over the moon that Sourcebooks became the source for this give-back launch. Working with fabulously talented editor Shana Drehs, who saw an even higher reach for this book than I did, was a great experience. Thank you, Lindsay and Shana. It's been a privilege to work with you both.

On the home front, I thank my husband Jim and sons Evan and Jeff. As always, I greatly appreciate their support, encouragement, and good humor, especially in the final editing stretches. You guys teach me every day that being generous and giving back begin at home.

A special thanks to Teresa Funke, who shares the writing world experience with me and is beyond generous with her support and keen insights. And another resounding note of gratitude to Alexia Nestoria, whose wide-ranging knowledge of international volunteering and the give-back community was extremely valuable.

Introduction

The Opportunity of a Lifetime — Become an Agent of Change

"We can't say our generation didn't know how to do it. We can't say our generation couldn't afford to do it. And we can't say our generation didn't have reason to do it. It's up to us."

— Bono

"Never in my life have I felt such an easy sense of community," says Amanda Anderson-Green, a twenty-five-year-old medical researcher from Seattle who spent three weeks on a volunteer vacation in Ghana. Each morning, she loved walking along red-dirt roads lined with women and children who'd smile and greet her as she went to volunteer at a center with HIV-positive people and AIDS orphans. "I was struck by the simplicity of it. People talked with me as if I was their neighbor. They were so open, friendly, and accepting. They'd put their arms around me and thank me for coming."

Her thoughts often drift back to Ghana and the people who touched her. "I wonder a lot about the children at the orphanages," she says. "They were quite precious and would clamor for our attention, sometimes getting into arguments about who could sit in our laps."

She thinks especially about Sayram, a quick little boy who would come to study each night by the light of the volunteers' generator. He picked up card games easily, read very well, and was a math whiz. "I wonder what will become of a boy like him, who is so obviously hungry for knowledge and wanting to become someone great."

Anderson-Green's trip was sponsored by Cross-Cultural Solutions through Travelocity's Change Ambassadors Program (www.crossculturalsolutions.org). Now back in Seattle, she says, "I am still receiving the gifts from my trip. I knew I would have a rewarding adventure, but I had no idea how much going abroad would impact my views of community, happiness, and service here at home."

When John Heineman learned that more than forty-seven million Americans—including about eight million children—were stranded in the boat of having no health insurance, he took to the waters, literally. While attending the University of Iowa in Iowa City, Heineman volunteered at the Iowa City Free Medical Clinic. "I was shocked to hear that so many hardworking families relied on the clinic each year because they could not access the safety net of health insurance," he says.

A month after he graduated from the U of I in May 2007, and after intensive training, he swam the English Channel in twelve hours and forty minutes to raise money for the Iowa City clinic. He called his campaign Crossing for Care. "There is no bloody reason to attempt such a feat of idiocy," Heineman says. But once he did, he said he was able to "search the depths of [his] stamina," much like uninsured people are forced to confront theirs.

When she planned her sixth birthday party, Morgan Atwell of Evergreen, Colorado, told her friends to skip the presents. Instead, she urged them to pool their pennies so she could help support a school in the remote mountains of Pakistan and Afghanistan. So far, Atwell, the first-grade activist, has raised more than $700 for school supplies. She's one of legions of kids around the country whose pennies have gone to Pennies for Peace (www.penniesforpeace.org), a swift-growing arm of the Central Asia Institute. CAI has built sixty-four schools in Afghanistan and Pakistan, educating twenty-five thousand students, despite constant turmoil there.

Why would a little girl in the Rocky Mountains feel such a connection to kids living in the mountains of Taliban country? "I don't know. It just comes up in my mind, and it fills my heart with love," Atwell says thoughtfully.

The basic human impulse, beyond giving money away to a person who needs it, is wanting to make a change in the world."

—*Sara Engelhardt,*
president of the Foundation Center

But segueing quickly into savvy fund-raising mode, she asks, "I've heard that a penny buys a pencil. Do you know how much a pencil sharpener is?"

Something New Being Born

These three individuals represent a new uprising, as we rush to step into the gap between the developed and developing worlds, giving back all around the globe—and across the United States.

They and millions of their counterparts are powering a give-back movement no one saw coming: ordinary people, like you, me, your neighbor down the street, and your aunt in Ohio, going head-to-head with extraordinary poverty in the developing world, AIDS, malaria, illiteracy, the lack of safe drinking water, and tough challenges here at home—and having the time of our lives in the process.

> The Give-Back Solution is a phrase I use to describe the unprecedented surge of ordinary people choosing to step up and use their time, talents, and travel to make a better world. The world has never seen so many people, across all age groups, volunteering and supporting causes that serve the common good and bring much-needed hope and solutions across the earth. This Give-Back Solution is bringing out the best in us and changing the face of the world: we are choosing to remain hopeful, connected, and empowered—to take on the world's toughest challenges and transform them with generosity and collective goodwill.

Bill Draper, the head of Ashoka, a nonprofit that promotes social entrepreneurs across the world, says we are experiencing "the most profound historical transformation in the structure of society since the agricultural revolution—the shift from a world led by small elites to an 'everyone's a changemaker' global society."

This new story couldn't have come at a better time. Just when hopes may be dimming for some of the seemingly hopeless areas on Earth, when rich nations and governments appear to be falling short, private citizens are stepping in to write a dazzling new chapter in our global humanity. And they're reporting that they've never felt so alive, vibrant, and full of purpose.

Finally, people are thinking big, really big, and calling us to go there, too. Aware of our own good fortune, tired of waiting for entrenched, sluggish aid organizations to make a big-enough difference, we're rolling up our sleeves in remote villages that have been below our radar for far too long—and in our own communities around the country.

This is our time to be useful, our opportunity to serve the world with our gifts. We all can channel our inner Oprah, Bono, Brad, or Angelina and help lift up a piece of the planet. "If a soft drink can get to the far corners of the world, why can't we get our drugs and our bed nets there, too?" a World Health official once asked. Why not, indeed?

Ordinary people taking on the needs of the earth set in motion something we've not seen before: a grassroots force bringing a seismic resurgence of hope—with an intensity no one saw coming. The people-to-people connection we're hungry for is happening. Optimism is rising in far-off villages, neglected rain forests, and crude medical clinics, where babies are still born without a lightbulb, their mothers unable to see their faces for the first time. Hope is streaming into our own inner cities, pockets of poverty, schools, homeless shelters, and wilderness areas hurt by federal cutbacks. We're finally seeing—really seeing—people and problems that have been invisible for far too long.

Why Now?

Why are so many of us rushing to give back? Why is personal philanthropy tapping such a deep root? What brings so many people of all ages to remake their lives to volunteer in villages in the developing world or do outreach work from home, considering it not just a mind-blowing experience, but an amazing privilege?

Many believe we're seeing a humanitarian tipping point, as a critical mass of people conclude they can no longer sit still and watch more than twenty thousand people die each day from preventable diseases. Or sit by and see the world's environments decline further. "A strange and wonderful thing has happened to this country in the past few years," observes Jacqueline Novogratz, founder and CEO of Acumen Fund, a global nonprofit venture offering loans or grants for small businesses that boost the livelihoods of impoverished people. "There's been a surge of interest in individuals and the chronic problems of countries thousands of miles away.

"Perhaps the most important change? A growing sense that we're all interconnected," says Novogratz. Plus, this give-back solution brings out the best in us and gives the rest of the world a chance to see us in a different light. "Volunteers really are the best face of our country," says David Caprara of the Brookings Institution's Building Bridges Coalition, a powerhouse of 150 organizations, from Microsoft to Habitat for Humanity, that promotes volunteering overseas (www.wevolunteer.net).

Your Passport to Greater Joy

Giving back doesn't mean that you don't get anything in return. Helping others reach for a new day rejuvenates us in ways that another margarita-soaked vacation, more stuff, a fatter résumé, or a supersized house can't begin to. We want to feel useful. We want to find meaning. We want to know we matter. We want to feel this alive and on fire with possibility.

What could your piece of this give-back movement be? The entry points for engagement are exploding—and reaching out. What could yours be?

Ultimately, it's about how to find the right match for your passion—whether that means volunteering while on vacation, reaching out to local nonprofits with an international reach, tutoring kids in your city, helping launch a start-up company in the developing world, or donating medical supplies and aid. But admittedly, vetting the many options out there can be overwhelming without some guidance, research, and talking with other volunteers.

That's where this book can be your connection. Part down-to-earth research guide, part inspiration, part socially conscious call to action, *The Give-Back Solution* captures the renewal of idealism and hope sweeping our country. It demonstrates the amazing impact everyday volunteers can have and helps you choose the best give-back strategy for you—whether that means gallivanting and giving back via a volunteer vacation or making an equally powerful contribution right where you are, with your time, talents, and resources. Whatever you choose, you can profoundly affect a piece of the world—and rock yours in the process.

How This Book Can Help

Whether you're a newbie volunteer or a seasoned humanitarian, this book can help you volunteer for the first time—or engage again and again. In Part One, you'll learn how to better define your "benevolence bliss" and find the right matches for your passion and talents and visions. Thanks to a renaissance in many existing organizations and an explosion of new ones, like the burgeoning Without Borders groups, there's bound to be a match for your desire.

In Part Two, *The Give-Back Solution* showcases people, projects, organizations, and companies that can help you engage in the developing world—or make a difference here at home—and take on issues from AIDS and malaria to deforestation, pollution, and poverty. It shows how you can travel abroad, and it also shines a light on powerful, effective ways you can engage right where you are, without traveling. Through the power of the Internet and by connecting with organizations that already have a sweeping global reach, you can take on many challenges and often see the impact of your contribution.

For anyone who chooses to make a difference by going abroad, Part Three provides bookends to your travel experience: you'll read about what kinds of questions and concerns you may want to consider before you go, in addition to checklists to help you prepare, and you'll discover tips on how to re-enter the world once your trip is over.

Throughout the book, you'll find stories from volunteers who have been at the forefront of this giving movement, plus in-depth looks at organizations that are leading the way.

This book is about how to connect and help lift up, usually in partnership with, the amazing people living in poverty. It also shows ways you can support endangered animals, reforest lands, and conserve the environment in our country and in the developing world. It's up to you to decide where to go, how to serve, and what to experience.

My Own Epiphany

My work has been leading me to shine a light on this "everyone's-a-change-agent" moment for a long time. For fifteen years, I've written about humanitarians and their projects, which led me to talk with some of today's leading changemakers and peacemakers, including Jane Goodall, Mohammed Yunus, Arun Gandhi, former secretary of state Madeleine Albright, and others. I've volunteered for and worked with BeadforLife, a nonprofit working in Uganda, which you'll read more about shortly. I've written about the grassroots explosion of ordinary volunteers.

Then, I had an epiphany of sorts when I wrapped my latest book on peacemaking: it's the grassroots, bottom-up humanitarian efforts that will ease the root causes of poverty and stabilize the world. This realization totally spoke to me, excited me, and threw open the door to look at this give-back solution. The more I gathered in-the-trenches stories from people making peace from Bosnia to Columbia, some who had never before been interviewed, the more I came to understand one powerful truth: ordinary people coming together, face to face, heart to heart, to build cooperative relationships will create the global peace and well-being for which we all long. And I knew my next book would look at—and celebrate—the impact of citizen engagement around the world, as ordinary volunteers create this extraordinary, more connected, compassionate world that works for us all.

I plunged into that wider world not long ago myself. For years, I'd longed to go to Africa, and I actually started having dreams about being in Africa, dancing with African women. Hungry for more marrow in my work, and with our oldest son rebelling and ready to vault the nest, I saw a chance to spend two weeks capturing the stories of Ugandan refugees. And I grabbed it.

It felt amazing to know I could help shore up this beautiful part of the world when some of my own was on rapidly shifting ground. I went to Kampala to listen to the amazing women of BeadforLife, many HIV-positive war refugees, who ingeniously learned how to roll gorgeous, colorful beads from the only resource they had: recycled magazine pages.

Each day, for three years, the women had gathered to roll beads in the blazing sun outside their huts. Then, they stuffed the beads into black garbage bags, determined that the bracelets and necklaces would somehow make their way into the hands of American women.

THE POWER OF INTENTION IN ACTION

Their garbage-bag intentions were so strong, they attracted incredible treasure: some American women who just happened to be walking through the beaders' sun-baked slum one day and decided to not look away. Torkin Wakefield, Devin Hibbard, and Ginny Jordan passionately launched BeadforLife (www.beadforlife.org) to market the jewelry. Now the gorgeous necklaces, earrings, and bracelets in vivid "shouting colors," as the Africans call them, have magically made their way to eager women across the United States. Oprah has featured them. Top fashion models have sported them on runways. They were showcased in the famous 2007 *Vanity Fair* Africa issue, edited by Bono. And the three hundred amazing women of BeadforLife now support about three thousand others. An amazing success story—one of millions rippling across the earth right now.

THANK YOU FOR NOT SITTING ON YOUR SOFT CHAIR

Like Amanda Anderson-Green, who spent time in Ghana, I still think about the people I got to know, including a stunning woman named Rose. She'd told me that two years before, she was dying from AIDS. "Before I joined BeadforLife, I looked like a lady of eighty," she had said, sucking in her cheeks and hunching her body to illustrate how gaunt she once was. But when I met her, she radiated good health and hope. Looking like African royalty in an elegant, gold-trimmed, vivid rose-colored gown, Rose had known she had something big going on. "BeadforLife has brushed the dust off my soul!" she'd beamed.

Rose was not only vibrant again, but she had just opened her first ever bank account and was now able to send her four children and her sister's three children to school. Her sister died from AIDS. Only a few years before, Rose was rising at 5:00 a.m. and begging in the streets for money to try to support them.

Now she was a force to be reckoned with. She was well aware that a mountain of misery was perched just above us in the hillside slums of Kampala, where thousands of people struggled with malaria fevers, despair, and AIDS. Her home was once often miserable, too, she said. "But now if you would come to my house, you would see that we are a very happy family. You would think you would stay one hour, and four hours later, we would still be together, laughing," she said, clapping her hands with glee.

New gold shoes had glittered on Rose's feet, like a symbol of her new foothold in life. When she floated on them across the red earth, the air shimmered around her. I felt myself shimmer in her presence. I felt alive and firmly grounded in the world in a way I'd never felt before. "Thank you for not sitting on your soft chair in America and letting us die," Rose said, clasping my hands in hers.

"We are caught in an inescapable network of mutuality, clothed in a single garment of destiny. I can never be what I ought to be until you are what you ought to be, and you can never be what you ought to be unless I am what I ought to be."

—*Dr. Martin Luther King, Jr.*

Rose reinforced something I'd believed, but not always felt: we are here for each other. I felt like I'd finally come home, to myself, in the world.

INFECTIOUS IDEALISM EASES POVERTY

Rose is now happy, determined, and infectious—much like the people-powered philanthropy that's transformed her. This HIV-positive mother is proud of how she is facing down poverty and disease. She is also seeing a much brighter economic future.

Rose has three income streams—including caring for others with AIDS—and has branched off into making other jewelry. "With BeadforLife as my glasses, I am seeing very far!" she laughs.

Their project is indeed taking a bite out of poverty, but it feeds our poverty of spirit, too. The Roses of the world are seizing rich, abundant new lives, because ordinary people are taking our generosity to new heights.

You can be one of them.

Signs of the Give-Back Surge

Global activism is increasingly hot, relevant, meaningful, even hip. Volunteers aren't waiting for the World Bank, UNHCR, or UNICEF to change the world. They're diving in and doing it on their own time and terms and finding great satisfaction in the process. Lives are being saved, and hope is returning to people short on hope. Here are some barometers of the make-a-difference movement:

- Americans gave a record $295 billion to charity in 2006.
- A recent *USA Today* survey found that a staggering 61 percent of thirteen- to twenty-five-year-olds feel personally responsible for making a difference in the world.
- About one hundred thousand people are expected to take a volunteer vacation this year. More than fifty-five million have already participated in one. The University of California–San Diego found that

45 percent of Americans have considered volunteer vacations; 72 percent know someone who has taken one. The reasons for this uptick are as varied as the people of the world. Here's one volunteer vacation rep's take: "The 1960s were all about relaxing vacations; in the '80s, vacations were about being active or seeking adventures. Now, people are seeking meaningful vacations. People have a very quiet but desperate need to find meaning in their lives. After September 11, Americans became concerned about the way the world viewed the United States. Then natural disasters like the tsunami in Asia and Katrina caused thousands of volunteers to go and help out."

- Corporate giving to international concerns rose 13 percent in 2006.
- Giving circles, in which groups of people pool their resources and dedicate them to a chosen cause, are up 30 to 50 percent.
- Private philanthropic foundations rose 35 percent from 1999 to 2004.
- More for-profit companies, from Travelocity to Target, are combining philanthropy with their commercial enterprises. Seventy-two percent of Americans want employers to do more to support a cause or societal issue, say Bentley College researchers.
- Baby boomers are set to inherit about $41 trillion

over the next fifty years, and philanthropy experts at Boston College predict that much of that wealth will flow into "giving while living" philanthropy. "Giving while living" lets people set up foundations and charities while they're alive so that they're able to enjoy the impact of their work, whether that's putting up a school in Peru or offering a $100 loan to hardworking people in rural India.

PART ONE

Answering the Give-Back Call

How You Can Engage

"In a sense, the concept of 'us' and 'them' is almost no longer relevant, as our neighbors' interests are ours, as well. Caring for our neighbors' interests is essentially caring for our future."

—*The Dalai Lama*

CHAPTER ONE

Excavate Your Inner Humanitarian

What's calling you, pulling you in? What drew you to this book and its message? *The Give-Back Solution* can make it easier for you to help the world; it can also help you discover more about yourself and what you really want to contribute. It can help you show the world—and yourself—what you're capable of.

Maybe you already know what's compelling you to give back. Some people say they feel a sense of outrage or restlessness at the state of the world. Students say they've heard for years that this is their time to make a difference. Others refer to a moral, spiritual calling or keen sense of destiny, as if their entire lives were leading up to this opportunity to help others.

Lots of empty nesters say they've always wanted to venture out and give back for years, and now that the kids are gone, it's time to jet. They say that volunteering with those living on less than two dollars a day is the opportunity—and privilege—of a lifetime. Those who can't travel, but who are grateful for their good fortune and would like to share it with others, also want to engage right from their kitchens, offices, computers.

What's your dream? It costs nothing to dream—and everything not to. This is the time to dream, and dream big.

If you didn't let your fears, money worries, vacation time, or other limitations hold you back, what would you do?

Where do you turn when you're ready to engage for the first time—or again and again?

Consult Your Inner Compass

Africa kept calling me—for a long time. I just couldn't not do something. So by the time I finally arrived there and walked up the rocky, red-clay hillsides perched above Kampala, Uganda, and entered the beaders' ten-by-twenty-foot mud huts to listen to their stunning stories, it felt like coming home. It felt like an honor to witness what the beaders had survived.

Some of them barely escaped machete-waving rebels; some of them had walked hundreds of miles to safety, wounded or naked. Some fought to stay alive with AIDS after their families threw them out. These beaders had survived unthinkable torture and abuse, yet struggled with dignity and pride to survive and educate the children, including the orphans.

Most days, the unforgiving African sun would stoke the beaders' windowless homes into ovens long before noon. But soon I realized that just as much heat radiated off the women, who were on fire and leaving suffering, AIDS, poverty, and despair far behind. They were luminous with the knowledge that, with their own hard work, they were reaching for a new life and making enough money to feed their children, buy them medicines, and send them to school for the first time.

In two weeks, I got thoroughly hooked on making a difference in the developing world. As each day passed, I felt compelled to throw my notebook and recorders down and just be with the women and with professional storyteller Connie Regan-Blake, with whom I worked. Our stories merged, as sultry breezes moved through orange-blazing mango trees and noisy white cranes dipped and swayed on the wind overhead.

The beaders are discovering their place in our increasingly woven, wider world, one necklace and bracelet at a time. At the same time, we're each discovering our connection to each other.

FIGURING OUT *YOUR* CONNECTION

To better help you find your own connection in the wide world of give-back choices, consider these questions.

1. Listen to your give-back call. What's it saying and asking of you? Tune into your inner compass and see where it leads you. Trust your instincts, your hunches for what feels right. Perhaps for years you've been drawn to helping orphans in Africa or nurturing the sea turtles of Costa Rica. What comes instantly to mind?

2. What brings you here now? Why is this the right time to act? Has something happened to galvanize you? Were you shocked by a conversation about Darfur around the watercooler at work—or do you have a year off before you start college and want to see a piece of the world while doing a bit of good? Are you recently retired or searching for meaning after years in what feels like a dead-end career? Why now?

3. Are you drawn to a particular part of the country or of the world? Is there an area or region that's particularly compelling to you? Do you want to build a trail in a national park, ease poverty in Appalachia, or tutor kids down the street? Or is there a continent or culture calling you? Can you narrow down the country or region you'd like to support?

4. Do you want to roam? How in-the-trenches and hands-on do you want to be? Do you want to go and volunteer in a developing country for weeks, even months? Are you already feeling the adrenaline rush, knowing an adventure awaits? Do you feel like one foot's already on the soil of a Brazilian village or hiking in Tibet?

5. Do you want to make an impact—right where you are? Is hands-on work in the trenches of Asia or Africa a turnoff for you? Do you feel more concerned about and drawn to helping out your local community or your country? Are you seeing signs of greater poverty, environmental problems, or educational gaps in your own backyard? Maybe you want to step up your volunteering here before you branch out overseas? Does it feel right to make a powerful contribution by raising your voice, opening your wallet, or working for change, right where you are?

One Volunteer's Journey: Making a Difference at Home

After graduating from college, Lindsay Saperstone wanted a better way to connect herself to her Portland community and to occupy idle time. She started shopping around for a nongovernmental organization (NGO) that met her personal interests, one that was established so she could jump aboard as a volunteer with little experience. "I attended a few community groups' meetings and came across an ad on Craig's List asking for a volunteer willing to help organize one nonprofit's database. I was familiar with the software they use, so I responded to the ad."

Saperstone decided to volunteer for Voz (www.portlandvoz.org), a Portland group that deals with immigrants' rights. Voz empowers immigrant workers, particularly day laborers, to gain control over their working conditions and to exercise their collective power to address the issues they face.

The job, which consists of entering names of volunteers and donors into a database, is a perfect match for her, Saperstone says. "It furthers a cause I feel passionate about. Plus, I have always been extremely interested in learning about issues facing immigrants in the United States and have wanted to get involved with a group that is so vastly undersupported by society."

Saperstone also speaks Spanish, so her work allows her to practice the language. She finds it rewarding to know that she's helping Voz better organize the other volunteers who ask to join them each week. "It doesn't take much time and it means a lot to me," she says. "It is something anyone can do if they keep their eyes open."

6. Do you want to get up close and personal? Are you sensing the people and feeling the pull of connection? Is it necessary for you to work closely with the people you'll support?

7. Do you want an ongoing sense of community? Are you looking for a way to give back—and find camaraderie and a sense of community at the same time? Many people enjoy volunteer work for the sense of belonging to something bigger than themselves, plus the chance to connect on a more meaningful level with kindred people in our often isolated, frenzied lives.

8. Do you want to find a group or organization with similar values and aims before you make a commitment? Is it important to you that you hold the same ideals and vision? Do you find it more desirable to support a faith-based or religious organization with a stated mission? Or do you prefer a secular one?

9. Do you have a particular skill or sensibility you want to offer? Do you want to use your given profession to make a difference or feel you have a talent or gift that will lift up a part of the world? What's your personality like? There are no accidents in the world. We often possess just the right talents, strengths, and sensibilities to make things happen in the world. Central Asia Institute director Greg Mortenson

was a six-foot-six, physically active climber, raised by adventurous parents who moved the family to Ethiopia to give back when he was young. He later did trauma nursing in San Francisco ERs and often lived out of his car to save money. So when he felt compelled to rewrite his life to build schools in the rugged, remote mountains of Pakistan and Afghanistan, his experience, endurance, skills, and characteristics were invaluable. What uniquely suits you for the work you may choose? What you bring to the table doesn't have to be grandiose; it just has to feel right to you.

Why Give Back?

Don't give back to:

- Pad your résumé.
- Impress your girlfriend, boyfriend, employer, or school admissions counselor.
- Please your minister, parents, rabbi, or therapist.
- Fix a broken relationship.
- Make yourself feel better than "those poor people."
- Escape from an unworkable job.
- Meet hot girls/guys in exotic lands.
- Ease your guilt.
- Get away from an untenable home situation.
- Save souls.
- Get your parents, school counselor, or truant officer off your back.
- Save the world.

Do give back to:

- Grow into a fuller person.
- Gain a deeper appreciation of all the amazing people and creatures with whom we share this planet.
- Immerse yourself in another culture.
- Ease a little piece of suffering and poverty.
- Work for greater harmony, equality, and prosperity for all.
- Serve people living with dignity and determination.
- Become a more engaged citizen of the world.
- Feel satisfied and fulfilled.
- Better understand your own country and its relationship to the rest of the world.
- Develop friendships with your neighbors.
- Gain a respect for other cultures, languages, customs, celebrations, and beliefs.
- Join in the transformation of the world.
- Create more oneness.

10. Is there an issue that's captured your heart? Are you drawn to addressing a particular social, environmental, or economic challenge? Are you hoping to ease the suffering of war refugees, abused women, AIDS patients, tsunami survivors, or endangered animals? If an issue calls to you, there's sure to be an organization addressing it.

11. How flexible, nonjudgmental, and open-minded can you be? If you're choosing to go abroad, are you curious

about other cultures? Can you hang onto your Western sensibilities—part of who you are and what brings you to this work—but be open to the richness of other worlds? If you're working with impoverished, struggling people here, can you be not only accepting, but respectful? (More about this in "Ensuring a Safe, Successful Trip," page 221.)

12. Do you need external praise and rewards? Or can you be content with the internal satisfaction and knowledge that you made a difference? Can you stay upbeat and on task even when you're working independently and feedback from others is scarce or even nonexistent? Can you rely on your own core strength to carry you through when the going gets rough—or unexpected surprises crop up?

13. Do you have the patience to go the distance? Whether you're volunteering overseas or engaging here, sometimes things don't move as fast as we'd like. Are you okay if progress comes slowly, if some days the volunteering feels exhilarating, but other days it feels exhausting, even insignificant? It can take a long time to see notable changes in areas of the world untouched for decades, if not centuries. It can also take a long time to see

"The world needs ideas so novel that people might try to shoot them down."

— *Tachi Yamada,*
the Bill and Melinda Gates Foundation

What would you do today if you didn't shoot yourself down?

changes in your own town or the impact of your work on a conservation and wildlife project, for example.

14. Do you have what it takes? Do you understand that while humanitarian activism has become hot, it's not a halfhearted choice? If you long to do a volunteer vacation, are you ready to get your immunizations, malaria nets, and hiking boots? Do you have good health and endurance, especially for the more strenuous opportunities? Are you up to the emotional and physical challenges? If the volunteering is physically rugged, emotionally raw, and extremely unpredictable—at least some of the time—can you be okay with that? What if some of the work is more routine than exciting, more tedious than fast-paced? If you're an adrenaline junkie, can you dial it back?

15. Are you ready to live at a deeper level? Are you ready for the adventure to begin? Any time you step up and help someone else, whether it's an ailing manatee or a father longing to own a herd of sheep to help his family survive, your heart's taking a leap of faith, and you'll be connecting with others more intimately. You'll get to know people on a more profound, real level—and they will get to know your true nature, too.

On sale days, the Ugandan beaders proudly stepped from their huts and brandished swollen baskets of their beaded jewelry, from pale pinks and turquoises to bold greens, reds, and purples. As they waited to sell their creations, they freely shared their stories, dreams, fears—and sometimes dished up the gossip of the day. Do you want to have this kind of relationship with the people you serve?

If this feels too intimate or uncomfortable to you, no worries. You may be more suited to lending your talents and time to help raise funds, do valuable research, find software and computing solutions, maintain a website, or do other tasks for nonprofits, which are usually desperately in need of people with great skills—financial to business to analytical. You can powerfully support people in the developing world right where you are, however you feel called. There are many ways to do good, and that's the magic of this give-back time.

"Tracking lions in Kenya for eight hours a day requires patience and mental and physical stamina. It can be tough to head out at 3:00 a.m., navigating bumpy terrain in a Land Rover. But when you finally meet that predator face to face, what could be more wonderful?"

—*Earthwatch director of volunteer outreach,*
James Fry

THAT HELPERS' HIGH: VOLUNTEERING MAKES YOUR HEALTH AND SPIRITS SOAR

However you choose to share your talents and time, you'll get to enjoy the bone-deep, feel-good euphoria that always comes from helping others. Eleven-year-old Scott Tribbey, my nephew in Iowa, experienced that in the summer of 2008. One day, as the floodwaters rose on the University of Iowa campus and throughout his community, Scott and his longtime friend Joe Britton were playing games on their Wii and PlayStation.

"But then we got bored. So we decided to go and pitch in and help fill sandbags." Scott says. "It's no fun just to just gawk at the flood and just sit there and not do anything to help. It was actually pretty fun helping our community get through this."

Scott and Joe and their dads jumped on a bus that took them to a meeting place in Iowa City, where volunteers streamed in to fill sandbags. "We worked for about four hours and made about forty-five sandbags," Scott recalls. "It was really fun. Joe and I talked about baseball, which took our minds off the work and made it even more fun. Afterward, he stayed over at my house for a sleepover."

Scott says that helping out gave him a better sense of what was happening in his city to deal with the flood. "And it made me really proud of my community," he adds.

As Scott discovered, volunteering, even in the midst of a natural disaster, can feel amazing. If you're hooked on giving back, you're all over this, too. Truth is, we experience a full-on, undiluted rush of what it means to be human when we give to others. Who wouldn't like to feel calmer, more energized, or just plain satisfied more of the time? Do you find yourself wishing you had more optimism, better relationships—or were at least more at peace with yourself? And what about joy, juice, zest for living?

All these things come alive in us when we give back to others. Says Stephen Post, author, with Jill Neimark, of *Why Good Things Happen to Good People,*

"There is no better exercise for your heart than reaching down and helping to lift someone up."

—*Bernard Meltzer*

"You wish to be happy? Loved? Safe? Secure? You want to turn to others in tough times and count on them? You want the warmth of true connection? You'd like to walk in the world each day knowing that this is a place of benevolence and hope? Then I have one answer: give. Give daily, in small ways, and you will be happier. Give, and you will be healthier. Give, and you will even live longer. Generous behavior shines a protective light over the entire life span."

When we choose to give back, our entire being undergoes a feel-good transformation at the cellular level, scientists say, which fortifies everything from our psychological outlook to our heart and immune system.

Scientists refer to this feel-good phenomenon as the "helper's high." It even shows up in MRI brain scans.

No wonder, researchers say, we're intrinsically wired to give back after all. Giving back is the most natural, expansive impulse we have, which is why it boosts our health, satisfies our souls, even lightens our sleep. Doing good for others is just who we are and one of our most enduring instincts, from cradle to grave.

"If this is true, then a certain amount of selflessness ought to be wired into the very circuits of our brain," reported the *New York Times* in 2007. And that is just what researchers at the University of Oregon found in a recent study. Nineteen students were given $100 each and told that they could anonymously donate a portion of this money to charity. The students who, on average, donated the most showed heightened activity in the pleasure centers of their brain as they gave up the money. Their generosity was accompanied by a neural "warm glow."

Torkin Wakefield, founder of BeadforLife, believes as we ease poverty around the world, we also ease our own poverty of spirit. "I find living in the United States, just taking care of my own career and house, is too narrow for me. I need this aliveness," says Wakefield. She and her husband, Dr. Charles Steinburg, an AIDS doctor who trains Ugandan physicians and students, expected to stay in Africa four months. They're now going on their fifth year, after getting hooked on the juice of making a difference.

"I just felt energized. We were so caught up in this energy of helping that it was like a buzz—like a spiritual buzz."

—Lelani Clark,
after one week of volunteering

None of the altruism, anecdotes, or data is surprising to my friend Joan Borysenko. A Harvard-educated medical scientist and psychologist, bestselling author, and pioneer of integrative medicine, Borysenko says service is so healthy because it keeps us from fixating on ourselves. "Service creates a big base around narcissism. We think a lot less about ourselves and our troubles. Therefore, service is medicine. There's no question about that," she says. "For most of us, the flow of our thoughts and feelings is about ourselves: Am I happy? Am I comfortable? The Center for Purposeful Living says service reverses the flow of our thoughts so we're thinking about others, and that is so liberating." When I spoke with Borysenko on the first day of spring, she and her husband, Gordon Dveirin, were just back from a three-week pilgrimage to Dharmsala, India, to meet with his Holiness the Dalai Lama. He calls giving back or service "wise selfishness."

Sometimes we forget this, thinking that service is a one-way street, Borysenko says: "It's not like 'I, privileged white woman from my upper-middle-class background, can help you.' It's not like that at all. We get so much back."

"If giving weren't free, pharmaceutical companies could herald the discovery of a stupendous new drug called 'Give Back'—instead of 'Prozac'—and run TV ads about love."

—*Stephen Post and Jill Neimark, authors of* Why Good Things Happen to Good People

Volunteers often come with a refreshing, new perspective and a sense of clarity about their lives. That's what my intern, Lindsay, found after volunteering in Sri Lanka: "My passion to work for the betterment of third-world countries was reignited, and I returned to the United States with a whole new outlook on life. I am so grateful to have had this experience, which has not only strengthened my commitment to people living in poverty, but has made me a stronger person as well."

Research shows people who help others are way happier and healthier. Borysenko and Dveirin together wrote *Your Soul's Compass,* which features the collective wisdom of twenty-seven spiritual sages, Christians to Shamans, Buddhists to Quakers, and is sweet manna for any soul. Knowing the wisdom of this stellar group was still with her when we spoke last spring, I asked her a question that often nags me when it comes to making a difference, whether that's caring for the earth or a far-flung village: how can we give back without getting sucked into the fear-based perception that the world's in terrible shape and needs drastically to be fixed?

"The earth is without end, constantly evolving and constantly revealing itself," Borysenko replied. "It's not about fixing the earth, but about seeing what's possible when we all act together. And when we all act together, we bring a degree of harmony, beauty, and love to the world that wasn't present before here. As Rachel Naomi Remen says, we serve life not because it's broken, but because it's holy."

If you'd like to supplement spiritual wisdom with scientific data to better understand why giving back is so therapeutic, you don't need to look far. More research emerges continuously. Here are some studies that shine a light on what you innately sense each time you do good. Service, as Borysenko says, is medicine.

- Boston College research found that pain, depression, and disability in chronic pain patients decreased after volunteering. Participants also reported themes of "making a connection" and "a sense of purpose" when volunteering.
- Depression is eased by volunteering, found University of Texas researchers.
- The University of Miami found that long-term survivors of AIDS were significantly more likely to have volunteered—especially in helping others with HIV.
- Volunteering even helps you live longer, according to University of California–Los Angeles researchers. "A generous spirit may yield generous life span," said a *USA Today* headline of the findings.

- And for kids, who have their whole lives ahead of them, the benefits of giving back are also rosy. Numerous studies show that teenagers who get turned on by service learning and volunteer work are much happier and more optimistic, compassionate, and open to new experiences in the future. They also get better grades, use drugs less, and are "other-centered"—which helps them navigate the stresses of being a teen. A 2004 study of thirty-one thousand Vermont teens found that voluntourism trips are closely linked to avoidance of risky behaviors.

Interesting—just reading the good news about giving back is making me feel better. How about you?

CHAPTER TWO

Channeling Your Passion

The Many Give-Back Options

Now you likely have a keener sense of what makes your humanitarian heart tick and how you might want to dive in and volunteer, whether that means getting malaria nets to mothers in Kenya or reaching out to at-risk kids in San Diego. As you think about what part you can play in making a better world, take a look at this overview of the kinds of organizations and give-back campaigns out there.

As you'll see, you can engage with any of them from home by volunteering locally, virtually, or domestically. You can impact the globe from your computer—or you can go and give back anywhere in the world.

Finally, the resource section at the end of the book offers a representative listing of organizations from all of these arenas, which will embrace your passion, service, and idealism. Also, at any point in your search for the right volunteering or service opportunity, check out a great online resource, Idealist, created in 1995 by Action Without Borders (www.idealist.org). This online clearinghouse helps you find volunteer opportunities, service and community-action events—and paid service positions—around the world. You can create a profile with your interests, and Idealist will match you with existing volunteer opportunities.

Idealist also offers global volunteering fairs and online resource centers to help individuals make informed decisions about service. A resource center specifically focused on international service is just coming online, says Erin Barnhart, Action Without Borders/Idealist manager of volunteerism initiatives.

Nonprofits, Nongovernmental Organizations, and Not-for-Profits

From small family foundations to large international nonprofits, from the growing Without Borders groups to social organizations like Kiwanis and Rotary International, a growing number of nonprofits are addressing humanitarian issues and serving the public good. Family foundations alone have spiked 77 percent in the past ten years, according to the Foundation Center. If you have a cause you want to champion, there's sure to be a slew of nonprofits leading the way, many of which are in your own community. (Many volunteer-vacation groups featured in this book are also nonprofits, but not all are.)

For-Profit Companies

Corporate giving and volunteering programs are on the rise, as are for-profit companies that offer humanitarian services or products, including volunteer vacations. Ten years ago, international corporate volunteering didn't really exist. Now, two out of every five major companies support employees' volunteer activities around the world. Many businesses make a difference in their own communities and support employees' give-back choices. Doing good is now an expected—and exciting—business strategy.

Government Agencies

The U.S. government offers both domestic and international volunteering opportunities through well-known organizations like the National Park Service, the Peace Corps, United Nations Volunteers, and other groups. You could also help the growing number of disabled veterans by serving at a veterans administration hospital.

Volunteer-Vacation Providers

Volunteer vacations are offered by both nonprofits and for-profit companies. According to the Building Bridges Coalition (see box, p. 24), at least eighty thousand Americans are choosing a volunteer vacation or excursion abroad as their passport to joy, fueling what's called "voluntourism."

Voluntourism combines a vacation or trip with volunteering on local projects that immerse you in the local culture. Interest in and opportunities for voluntourism, both domestically and internationally, are getting hotter all the time. On many of the trips, you'll give back and then have time to adventure and play, mixing service and relaxation in gorgeous parts of the world. Other volunteer stints, both domestically and abroad, are much more focused on the volunteering, with little time to roam and relax.

Nearly a quarter of Americans are interested in taking a volunteer vacation, says the Travel Industry Association of America. Condé

Nast and MSNBC say it's actually higher: they found that 75 percent of respondents have taken a volunteer vacation or want to.

Travelocity says that 38 percent of more than a thousand survey respondents are interested in taking a vacation where they can give back and make a difference. Travelocity employees created its Travel for Good program as a way to better the world through travel. One component of Travel for Good: $5,000 Change Ambassadors Grants, like the one used by Amanda Anderson-Green for a volunteer vacation, including trip accommodations.

Building Bridges Coalition Boosts Volunteers Abroad

If you decide to go abroad for your volunteering, you'll have ample company. By 2010, the Building Bridges Coalition, a consortium of 150 organizations, aims to see a hundred thousand volunteers abroad.

The Coalition brings together leading international volunteer organizations, universities and colleges, corporations, and government agencies to boost the number of volunteers abroad each year, improve the quality of its service, and maximize the positive impacts of international service around the world.

Its members range from Pfizer to Habitat for Humanity to American University to the State Department.

Steven Rosenthal, executive director of Cross-Cultural Solutions and Building Bridges Coalition chairman, tells us more about his organization.

Q: What age groups are volunteering most now?

A: We see three different brackets. First are the college students, new graduates, or gap-year students who want to volunteer before entering university. At the other end of the spectrum are those just retired or between jobs or empty nesters, who are literally calling us when the nest is still warm as they come back from dropping their kids off at school. In the middle are young professionals in their thirties who volunteer for a week or two, maybe before they have kids. Many people say they see volunteering as the opportunity of a lifetime. We hear things like, "I've always wanted to do this; now I finally can."

"College students today are not only going abroad to study in record numbers, but they are also going abroad to build homes for the poor in El Salvador in record numbers or volunteering at AIDS clinics in record numbers. Not only has terrorism not deterred them from traveling, they are rolling up their sleeves and diving in deeper than ever."

— *Tom Friedman,*
New York Times

One commonality we see among the volunteers: they're often in transition. If you're in a time of personal transformation, volunteering gives you a new perspective of things back home.

But don't overlook another demographic: young professional women. They might be traveling less, especially if they have young children, but they are as turned on and tuned in to international issues as anyone else. They might be aware consumers, speak with their checkbook, engage in philanthropy, and be active microfinance donors, but not have the time to volunteer abroad right now. But they are right up there when it comes to engagement.

Q: *Why are so many people volunteering now?*

A: With the globalization of the world, we see more of what's going on. We understand how much smaller the world is. We see that people on the other side of the planet are living on less, and it's become easier and easier to help them. Take microfinance (see chapter seven). Most people have the ability to extend a $25 loan to a new enterprise somewhere.

Ultimately, what we're seeing right now is all the outside factors of the last seven years really coming to a head. September 11 caused us to become more globally aware of the fact that events around the world affect us back home. The war in Iraq also caused the image of the United States to spiral downward, causing Americans to feel more passionate about engaging overseas to counteract that image of them.

Q: *David Caprara, director of the Brookings Institution's Initiative on International Volunteering and Service (and member of the steering committee for the Building Bridges Coalition) said that "volunteers show the best face of America." Do you agree?*

A: I definitely agree with that statement. That's what we're seeing overseas. We often hear people in our communities overseas say, "We got to know more of what Americans are like. We see the actions of the U.S. government, and we recognize that its people are quite different. People are all one, and this volunteer showed me we're all the same." Grassroots diplomacy comes across through international volunteering. International volunteering absolutely puts the best face of this country forward.

Q: What do you see ahead on the volunteering landscape?

A: I think we're entering a new era where people feel engaged and empowered to make a difference and have a lot of energy to turn around what's been happening the last seven to eight years. More people are getting involved on a broad scale and taking action. Volunteering abroad is growing like we've never seen before, and it holds so much promise. Ten years ago, it was much more challenging to get people to understand the importance of this. Now we have a common vocabulary and a consensus of what's important. People are motivated, activated, and energized, so in the next five years, we'll see much more engagement and many more volunteers. They are concerned about what's going on on the other side of the world. They want to see the fulfillment of John F. Kennedy's vision: one million volunteers overseas, active, aware, and moving public policy in the right direction. One million people with an expanded worldview, making a substantial impact on the world.

Q: Can ordinary volunteers really impact the tough issues—or do we just get a quick feel-good fix?

A: Is international volunteering a cure-all for poverty? Absolutely not. Can it make a positive impact? Absolutely. Washington University is studying the long-term impact of volunteers and finding that volunteers have a very positive, substantial impact. You also can't overlook the long-term impact of volunteers when they go home. They keep on engaging in global issues. They rethink their careers, dinner-table conversations, and spending patterns. They go on to have much more engaged lives in response to what's happened to them overseas. That means eighty thousand people will come home and make new decisions about how to live their lives and impact poverty.

For more info: Building Bridges Coalition: www.wevolunteer.net

Giving Circles: An Easy Way to Transform the World, Right Where You Are

If you want to address some of the biggest issues here and around the world—without leaving home—consider one of the growing numbers of giving circles. Giving circles bring communities of people together, either in person or online, to pool their donations for a specific, agreed-upon project or cause. It's a brilliant way to change the world and meet kindred people in the process.

Here's one woman's electrifying giving circle that's spreading nationwide.

Marsha Wallace, a nurse in South Carolina, was restless with her work, "earnestly searching for my path," she says. She wanted to help people around the world but wasn't sure where to start.

One night in 2003, Wallace was meditating, and she was

jolted "like an electrical shock" by an idea. She quickly called twenty-five friends and hosted a unique potluck. What if they pooled the money they would have spent dining out and sent it instead to a women's project in the developing world, Wallace asked them. The women loved the idea, and they collected $700 that night for Women for Women International (www.womenforwomen.org).

Dining for Women (www.diningforwomen.org) was launched around that table, and Wallace was convinced women everywhere would love the idea. But they didn't at first. Not only did it not catch fire right away, but Wallace was afraid it might sputter out entirely. Then after a 2005 article in *Woman's Day*, interest surged. "The *New York Times* called, and *Good Morning America* came to my house and filmed part of a dinner here," Wallace recalls. "I was so excited, I was squealing. This has been more exciting than anything I've ever done."

In a recent mailing to her supporters, Wallace wrote, "I didn't envision what Dining for Women has become. I simply wanted to raise money for women internationally and have fun with my girlfriends!"

That fun has evolved into 2,200 Dining for Women members in 95 chapters around the country, who've collectively raised $117,700—one meal at a time—for projects around the world. "In the process, we've learned about important issues facing women all over the globe, including health care, education, human-trafficking prevention, human rights awareness, maternal and child health care, food stability, microcredit, and vocational training," Wallace says.

She anticipates a feast of donations ahead. Women keep contacting her with novel ways to form their own chapter. Second-year medical students in Atlanta, for instance, gather on Thursday nights to watch *Grey's Anatomy* over pizza and pool their Dining for Women donations.

Wallace went on her first trip to India in 2007 to see the impact of Dining for Women's support, but she shows what can be done right where we live—and eat: "My ultimate goal is to change the face of poverty for women worldwide. There are so many women with expendable income, if we could all band together, we could be a huge force with which to be reckoned."

Online Campaigns

Many successful give-back initiatives are launched largely online by individuals or organizations, often with great word-of-mouth buzz and media exposure. This form of giving back appeals to people who want convenience, immediacy, and a sense of belonging in our digital, connected world. Online giving totaled $250 million in 2002. It was up to more than $4.5 billion in 2005, according to ePhilanthropy Foundation. Consider one of the most magical online campaigns: Oprah's Angel Network, which has raised millions and supported everything from Habitat for Humanity houses to schools in Africa (www.oprah.com). Anyone with an inspirational idea can rally hundreds—even millions, in Oprah's case—to lift up a piece of the world. Students' Facebook campaigns, viral marketing, and online giving challenges, like those done at the Case Foundation (www.casefoundation.org), all spark new ways to care and connect.

Celebrate the Progress in the World

As you'll see in this book, when it comes to describing the volunteer opportunities, the experiences, and the global challenges they address, I don't talk about "fighting" or "defeating" anything, whether it's AIDS, illiteracy, malaria, or deforestation.

Attacking, waging war, and trying to defeat what we don't want in the world doesn't work. Changing our focus to imagine and reach for what we truly want to see in the world? That does work, brilliantly. "Change your focus from what needs to be torn down to what needs to be built up," says acclaimed peacemaker William Ury, who's not fighting against the conflict in the Middle East, but helping create an unprecedented path there—the Abraham Path, which allows people to meet one another and find common ground as they walk in the footsteps of the prophet Abraham (www.abrahampath.org).

We're called to be aware of and to respond to the challenges and injustices on the earth, whether it's the lack of clean water for too many or the rising tide of AIDS orphans. This book absolutely acknowledges that almost unimaginable suffering exists, like what Beadfor-Life member American Height endured. She says that rebels killed her parents as her grandmother tried to shield her and her brothers. The rebels warned that they would come back, and they did. They later killed both boys. Knowing she had to escape or be killed, American

Height somehow managed to flee on foot and made it hundreds of miles away to Kampala. And joined thousands of other refugees.

Almost paralyzed by grief, jobless, depressed, and sick, she tried to get ahead by working in a rock quarry, sitting in the blistering sun with no food, just small amounts of water, smashing rocks with a tiny mallet. For a dollar a day.

These are the stark realities for too many people on Earth.

But it doesn't have to stay that way. We can see the atrocities, become aware, and respond as never before. That means we have to shine a greater light on the rising opportunities to build something greater, whether it is through nonprofits helping the world's refugees, like Refugee International, corporations sponsoring employee volunteer projects abroad, the U.S. government's Peace Corps, or one of the many volunteer-vacation organizations such as Global Volunteers (www.globalvolunteers.org) and Projects Abroad (www.projects-abroad.org).

This book is all about visionary ideas, unprecedented programs, and rigorously vetted and tested workable solutions that can and are transforming the world.

Together we can create something new on Earth that isn't possible when we work alone. Or when we work out of despair and fear. So with that in mind, here's some good news.

The *Economist* recently published an article sharing statistics about how the world is doing in three categories: the underlying social condition in poor countries, poverty alleviation over the past decade, and the incidence of wars and political violence.

- Twenty-five years ago in China, over 600 million people were living on less than a dollar a day. Today this number is 180 million, meaning that 420 million are now above this level.
- Between 1999 and 2004, 135 million people worldwide rose from less than a dollar a day to above this level. "This is more people, more quickly than at any other time in history," the *Economist* states.
- In South Asia, the number of people without clean water has been halved since 1990, when more than 25 percent of people in developing countries lived on less than a dollar a day. At current rates, this will drop to 10 percent by 2015, the magazine believes.
- A study shows that the number of conflicts (international and civil) fell from over fifty at the start of the 1990s to just over thirty in 2005. The number of international wars peaked in the 1970s and has been falling ever since. The death toll in battle fell from over two-hundred thousand a year in the mid-1990s to below twenty thousand in the mid-2000s.

Keep focusing on the good news if that's what you

want to see in the world. Be the change and be grateful for what's already happening. It's big; it's huge; and it's transforming life as we know it. And you can be a part of it.

CHAPTER THREE

How to Navigate Volunteering in the Developing World

Taking a Trip with Purpose

At this point, you may be pumped to join the rising tide of voluntourists rushing overseas to give back and make a difference.

Many believe voluntourism is gaining traction because celebrities, including Bill and Melinda Gates, Warren Buffet, Bono, and so many others, have focused laser light on the power of philanthropy in resource-poor nations. *Travel and Leisure's* take: "The rise of volunteer vacations seems to be the product of a serendipitous alignment: 10 to 15 years ago, at the same time that trips abroad became easier and less expensive and better-traveled Americans began to seek out more unusual travel experiences, volunteering also became the stuff of national conversation." The magazine cites the nonprofit organization Independent Sector, which found that 70 percent of volunteers do it to gain a new perspective on things.

Virginia Tech professor Nancy McGehee studied voluntourists' motives and found four major drives: They really want to "see real people, their lives, and their everyday living environment," and they have a healthy curiosity about other people and places. They also want to "reach out to the less privileged. Many participants felt they had done well in life and wanted to give back" via a "trip with a purpose," McGehee reports. Third, voluntourists seek camaraderie with people who share the same interests and values.

Finally, volunteer vacationers also appear to be motivated by the "education and family-bonding opportunities" presented by volunteer vacations. Globe Aware's Catherine McMillan says her family's volunteer trip to a small Mexican village, Chalcatzingo, where they helped construct a house and build a water cistern, gave them a genuine appreciation for how the rest of the world lives. "One of the special things we did was to offer the community dental care. There were tons of people with rotten teeth, unable to eat and in severe pain," McMillan says. "I served as the interpreter for the dentist, and my five-year-old son, Elijah, and I were holding a patient's hand. He was a little boy about the same age as my son.

"When the dentist triumphantly pulled out a rotten tooth with an 'aha!' my son looked up at me and said, 'Mommy? Can I go and brush my teeth?' I haven't had to fight him on brushing his teeth ever since."

My fourteen-year-old son, Evan, and I were on board to do a volunteer vacation in Thailand for all these reasons and more. And when we heard that we could help people in villages as we meandered through the country, swam under waterfalls, and visited ancient Buddhist temples, we found ourselves doing the happy dance, knowing we'd soon be in the "Land of Smiles."

Every day blew our minds.

One day, we and the six other volunteers were swaying back and forth on the back of an old, rusty truck as it forded streams and lumbered up dense Thai hillsides, where tigers, barking deer, monkeys, snakes, peacocks, and many tropical birds make their home.

Our assignment: cook a meal over an open fire for remote hill tribes struggling to make it day by day. This was day nine of our fourteen-day volunteer vacation in Thailand, via the UK-based organization i-to-i (www.i-to-i.com), which was taking us across much of the country, ending in the islands off the southern coast.

Straining and grinding its gears one more time, the truck finally lurched over the crest of the hill, revealing the village in front of us. Many little feet running in the dust stopped; many faces turned, curious. Women looked out from behind simple bamboo buildings or leaned to look from a few taller, stilted homes set back in the trees. Clusters of kids, including two little girls dressed in brightly embroidered red and blue dresses, stared at us and drew closer. These were some of the Karang tribespeople who had fled across the border from Burma, their birthplace, fleeing conflict with the Burmese military government.

Eventually, Tong, our guide, herded us all back to start cooking the meal. As I chopped vegetables, I was startled by a dull "thunk thunk" and looked up to see Evan. Up to this point, he'd had an aversion to even my puniest cooking knives. Now he was raising what looked like a massive machete above his head and forcefully pulverizing chicken pieces on a crude, wooden chopping block, all the while laughing and joking with another volunteer, Patrick.

Soon, we started cooking the chicken in an ingenious, three-chambered cooking pot. Tong showed us how to make broth, add pork balls and packets of amazing spices, and stir in the chicken, vegetables, lemongrass, and onion. It turned out to be one of the best soups we tasted on the trip. The hungry kids drew closer.

Claire, a volunteer from the UK, Jen from Chicago, and I noticed one little girl, who was bold and sassy. This dark-haired little urchin kept coming back and poking us from behind or slapping Claire's legs. This little girl, I thought, is the face of this flatter world in which we're living. Her people have been semi-nomadic, constantly on the move. Maybe it will finally become easier for her to find and get more stability and opportunities. Maybe she won't have to suffer as much as her ancestors. As she darted in and out to tease us and run away, I realized how she was caught up in that centrifugal force that we all seem to be drawn into, more eager than ever to connect with one another and make this world smaller, even if it begins with poking and prodding a few strange-looking, dusty volunteers.

After saying our good-byes and hearing the kids sing, we headed back down the hillside. Soon, we met another small group on the path. They were more volunteers heading back up into the village—a visible symbol of the ongoing flow of volunteers into the developing world, ebbing and rising, gaining traction.

Volunteers can promote understanding and peace. But maybe just plain curiosity and interest in the rest of the world are leading you to plan a trip. Maybe you've always wanted to experience the African savannahs at sunset or watch one of the remaining leatherback turtles crawl triumphantly back to the ocean. If you can do good at the same time, the experience is even more attractive.

It can be daunting at first to sort through your options and select a trip. But you'll feel your world expanding even as you look at the choices, from local nonprofits to international volunteer-vacation groups. Here are some questions to make it easier and more manageable and give you the confidence that you're finding the right match for your interests and desires.

> As you choose your voluntourism opportunity, whether domestically or overseas, pay attention to your own instincts and judgment. If something doesn't feel right for you, it probably isn't. Be rigorous; be well informed. Don't book anything until you're satisfied you've gotten the right answers and volunteer placement for you.

These questions can help you query and interview the various organizations that sponsor volunteers abroad. Start early; scan their websites; and then talk personally with representatives of the organizations by phone. As you visit the different websites to look at your options, read past volunteers' experiences. Don't be timid about asking lots of questions, because this is your trip, and you want to make sure you find a placement or volunteer opportunity that gives you the experience you're seeking.

Questions to Ask Yourself

- What area of the world is most calling you? Do you want to teach a room full of eager kids in Nepal—or tackle poverty here? Have you always wanted to visit a specific area of the country or world and really get to know its amazing people?

- What do you want to experience? Who do you want to help? This is where you can tap into your childhood, dormant, or incessantly loud dreams. Do you want to excavate your lifelong vision of plunging into the Amazon, or helping pandas affected by the earthquake in China, or nurturing babies orphaned by AIDS? Do you see yourself pounding nails for a school in the developing world so girls can finally get the education they deserve, or tutoring a child remotely from the comfort of your own home? Maybe you can't wait to track and count exotic, endangered butterflies? Make sure you understand your motivations. Complete the following sentence: "I've always wanted to…"

- How long do you want to be gone? Some projects last a week; others are year-round programs with flexible start and end dates. A popular option is two weeks, which also allows for some touring in the area.

- How many hours do you want to work each day? Do you want to work part of the day or all day? Do you want to make sure your evenings are free? How do you want your days structured?

- Do you want enough spare time to tour a little and see the culture? Many projects give you the opportunity to do so as part of the volunteering, including working alongside local people, but see how much free time for gallivanting and touring you'll have, if that's important to you.

Some organizations have specifically designed their placements to provide a mixture of volunteering and cultural exchange, touring, etc.

- What kind of accommodations/lodging do you desire? Expect fairly spartan accommodations—many groups will put you up in modest hotels, hostels, or homes, though plusher digs are sometimes possible. But if you want to immerse yourself more in the culture and stay with a local family or go into the wilderness and sleep on a hammock in the jungle, all that can be possible, too, with the right placement.

- What can you afford? A volunteer placement can start at $600 and go up from there. But be mindful that it's totally acceptable to do some fund-raising among family, friends, and your "people"—most of whom would be delighted to support your plans. More voluntourists are passing the hat for their travel all the time. Some volunteer organizations can give you ideas for fund-raising.

- Do you want to work side-by-side with local people? There's no better way to get to know the world's amazing people than to spend your days together, creating new things. Many projects will already afford you this opportunity, since their work is always done in partnership with the local villagers or people, but clarify this point.

What else is important to you? These are some key questions to ask yourself, but you will likely have your own. Sit with yourself; focus on your vision of what you want your experience to be. Get really clear on what is calling to you, and do your research to find the best organization to make it come alive.

Questions to Ask Volunteer-Vacation Organizations

After her volunteer vacation to Ghana, Amanda Anderson-Green said, "I am still receiving the gifts from my trip." Anderson-Green's volunteer vacation to Ghana was with a leading volunteer-vacation organization, Cross-Cultural Solutions (CCS), as part of Travelocity's Change Ambassadors program. CCS is one of hundreds of volunteer-vacation organizations you can team with to do everything from teaching AIDS orphans to helping women in the developing world secure first-time jobs.

You can have just as positive a service experience, but you'll want to do everything you can to make it that way.

Because voluntourism is booming, organizations are popping up overnight. So do your homework; ask the right questions; look over the organizations thoroughly; and find a reputable match. Don't get discouraged if it takes longer than expected. It takes what it takes, and your comfort level, trust, safety, and ultimate enjoyment are worth it.

This isn't time to hold back or be hesitant. Ask:

- Can you tell me more about your experience and track record? (If you've chosen a specific country or region in which to volunteer, ask how much experience the organization has there.) How many volunteers have you supported over the years?

- I am thinking of going to (name your country). What are your flagship programs there?
- I am thinking of (name the specific type of volunteering you'd like to do, if you know). What are your top projects in that area?
- How long have you been working in those villages or communities?
- Who are your team members, country coordinators, and tour guides? How are they trained? How long have they worked with your organization?
- Can I talk with past volunteers about their experiences? Can you give me contact info for some? Can you share any written testimonials or alumni stories from the projects I'm eyeing?
- What's the cost of my trip? What services will my fees cover? Can I get a breakdown? Can you make any suggestions for how I can fund-raise my fees?
- How much guidance and support will I receive from your staff before and during my experience? What type of training or orientation will I receive—once I arrive and while on the ground there? (Be clear on what "guidance and support" might mean to you. If you're expecting a translator of the language and culture at your side at all times, that may not be possible, especially as your guides are also responsible for a wide variety of tasks, including transporting you safely from one location to the next.)
- How physical will my volunteering experience be? (Depending on your needs, you may want to inquire about

the topography, climate, lodging, dining, and other challenges.) Are heavy lifting, extensive walking on rough terrain, or other strenuous tasks are part of the experience?

- What specific work will I do? Can you describe some
  specific tasks and assignments I'll have and what a typical day might look like? (If this is where you envision
  tutoring schoolchildren but the assignment calls for
  you to paint school desks and clean latrines, make sure
  you fully understand the scope of the project. If the organization has a breakout of days on the trip to email
  you, that's perfect. And if you're going to many different projects in one longer trip, from orphanages to out-
  door cleanup efforts, you can also ask about the work
  required at various locations.)

- Are you a faith-based or secular organization or affiliated
  with any other umbrella or political groups? Do you have
  a stated mission? (Some volunteer-vacation organizations
  have religious or political agendas. You want to make sure
  you are in total synch with the organization's values, supported causes, and goals.)

- Are you a nonprofit organization? (This may or may not
  be important to you. If it is, then do clarify.)

- Where will I be staying and with whom? (Accommodations could range from "a castle with beds to a shack in
  the African bush to a community building or schoolroom,"
  says Amy Bannon, Volunteers for Peace staffer.) Will I be
  in hostels, hotels, private homes, tents—or a combination
  of these? Will they be comfortable, clean, and safe? With

whom will I share accommodations? What if I want to have a home stay with a local family and be more integrated into their community?

- What will our meals be like? Is the staff confident the food will be healthy and safe? Will we always have access to clean water? Will I be assigned any cooking and cleaning for our group on my off hours?
- How equipped are you to deal with a natural disaster, violent outbreak, or some other emergency?
- Is my trip tax deductible?
- Can I get college credit?
- What's the language barrier?
- Who will meet me at the airport and take me to my first destination? How will I spot them?
- Can I get a list of the other volunteers in my group? (Just in case you'd like to email them in advance.)
- Can I communicate in advance with my in-country coordinator if I have any additional questions?
- Does your organization have trained local staff, and if so, how much contact will I have with them once I arrive?
- Tell me all about the safety considerations. Are there any risks in this region? What kind of communications systems and safety and hygiene standards are at each site? How close will I be to the local hospital? Who will transport me there, if, God forbid, anything should happen?
- What about traveler's medical insurance? (Most organizations now strongly recommend you get it—or they often provide their own insurance package.)

- What immunizations will I need? What's the malaria risk?
- Can you accommodate my dietary restrictions?
- What if an emergency arises at home and I have to return early?
- How will I communicate with family and friends during my time abroad? Do you have an online journal or blog so I can stay in touch with them during my trip? Will we be close to cybercafes? Does it make sense to bring phone cards, or will we largely be in more remote areas?
- Can you tell me more about the local customs? Are there local beliefs, practices, considerations of which I should be aware? What about clothing, religious rituals, gender issues, etc.?

Red Flags: What to Look Out For

As you talk with different organizations and make your final decision, here are some red flags to watch out for:

1. The staff can't adequately answer or is impatient about answering your questions regarding safety, fund-raising support, dietary restrictions, or any other issue.
2. The organization has no financial transparency. It can't or won't provide a breakdown of how your fees are spent and how much money stays with the local community and projects.
3. You aren't allowed to talk with past volunteers. The organization can provide no references.

4. You are offered no pre-departure orientation or an orientation after you arrive.

5. You will have little or no on-the-ground support from your host organization, or it passes you off to another organization or subcontractor after you've arrived. You should have at least one in-country staff member per program who can support you and your volunteer group.

6. There is no clear, defined system to handle on-the-ground emergencies.

This example's an extreme one, but it does underscore why you want to thoroughly check out your organization's contingency plans for emergencies, from natural disasters to outbreaks of conflict. It's shared by my intern on this project, Colorado State University journalism student Lindsay Mitchell, who has a real passion for giving back.

One Volunteer's Journey: When the Unexpected Arises: My Sri Lankan Adventure

When I first arrived in Sri Lanka, I had no idea what to expect. I was there for a three-month internship with Asiana Education Development (AED), an amazing organization working to feed and educate impoverished children of the country.

It was the middle of the night when I arrived at the orphanage where I'd be staying. I'd been traveling for more than forty hours and was absolutely exhausted! I awoke the next morning feeling refreshed, excited to see my new home in the daylight. I gazed out the window at one of the most beautiful sights I have ever seen—the Indian Ocean waves crashing against the shores of the black-sand beaches of Sri Lanka. I now understood why they named the orphanage Samudra Sri, which literally means "beautiful place by the sea."

AED was founded over twelve years ago by an American from Seattle who took a business trip to Sri Lanka and saw the desperate need for education in the region. Since its inception, AED has built over eighty schools throughout the country as well as two large orphanages.

After the tsunami hit in 2005, AED's work was compounded by the struggle to rebuild and recover from the devastating loss of lives, buildings, and homes. Many of the children at Samudra Sri lost their families in the tsunami. Most of the kids had come from depressing poverty and hopelessness. But if there is one thing I learned about the people of Sri Lanka, it is that their spirits and hearts are remarkably strong. By simply receiving hot meals, the chance to go to school, and, most importantly, love and attention, these boys and girls were given happiness and hope for a brighter future.

Sri Lanka's been in a bloody civil war for over twenty years, creating tragedy, displacement, and major barriers to progress, especially in the northern and eastern parts of the country, where the Tamil Tiger rebels have developed a stronghold over the years.

I knew going into this internship that there was much

political strife. But I decided to go anyway, because it's long been safe for people working away from the rebel strongholds. I would be staying very close to the capital, where not much violence has been seen in recent years.

All that was about to change. One night I awoke to the loudest boom I have ever heard in my life, followed by several minutes of gunfire. Lying alone in my apartment, I had no idea what to think. I didn't dare venture outside, as the sounds were so loud it felt like they were right outside my door. I eventually fell back asleep, trying to convince myself it was just some fireworks or something. But when I went down to speak with the orphanage staff the next morning, my worst fears were realized. The sound had indeed been a bomb—two bombs, actually—that had been dropped from rebel aircraft only a few miles from where I was staying. One of the bombs hit in the town where I went to work every day, injuring many people and wrecking several homes. The gunfire I had heard was the Sri Lankan military's anti-aircraft firing into the air.

My heart sank. What did this mean? What was going to happen next? Was I really that safe after all? Should I go home early? I had only been in Sri Lanka for four weeks; I was not ready to leave. But in the end it was not up to me whether or not I stayed, as the government had stopped extending tourist visas, and I could no longer legally reside in Sri Lanka. After much struggle to get me on a flight out of the country, I boarded a plane a week later that would take me back to the other side of the world—almost two months earlier than planned.

My emotions ran high as the plane took off. A mixture of relief, sadness, and disappointment welled up in my heart. What got to me the most, however, was not how the escalation in the war had caused me to leave, but rather what this meant for the work of AED, the children at Samudra Sri, and Sri Lanka. During my stay, I had fallen in love with the beauty of the country and its people. They know real suffering and loss, but also real joy and hope. My heart goes out to them as I continue to hear stories of increased bombings and intense violence throughout the country.

Yet in the midst of immense poverty, a devastating natural disaster, and a twenty-year civil war, the resounding message I received from my visit to Sri Lanka was one of hope and inspiration for what's possible in the world.

PART TWO

Ways to Change the World and Change Yourself

How You Can Take on AIDS, Malaria, Deforestation, Illiteracy, and More

The next six chapters present a full spectrum of exciting ways you can become more engaged and energized—ways you can make a real difference for people now and for generations to come. This section discusses opportunities, vacations, and trips for volunteering abroad and in the United States in education, global health, the environment, microfinance, and peace and conflict resolution. And it showcases the momentum, scope, and humanitarian reach that ordinary volunteers can really have. Through the eyes and impressions of ordinary volunteers and change agents like you, it's clear that one person really can make all the difference.

At the end of each section, you will read about the endless ways you can give back, right where you are.

CHAPTER FOUR

Channel Your Inner Oprah

Educate the Children

"Education is the most powerful weapon which you can use to change the world."

—Nelson Mandela

Denver restaurateur Noel Cunningham is accustomed to satisfying the hunger of the political, sports, and media stars who line up at his upscale eatery. When Bill Clinton and an entourage walked through the door one evening, Cunningham, an electric Irishman, was in his element.

But the hunger of two thousand Ethiopian kids lining up to beg for one of only 160 spots in their first-ever school? That still really gets to him. "I saw older kids hunkering down behind the school's fence to look small enough to enroll in the beginning classes," Cunningham recalls of a trip to Yetebon, Ethiopia.

Cunningham and his wife, Tammy, have helped put up a library, dormitory, and school for a thousand students in Yetebon by supporting humanitarian powerhouse Project Mercy (www. projectmercy.org). "Some of the kids were orphaned by AIDS and were living in a cowshed. They were grateful, because they at least had a cow to keep them warm. But now, every time we go there, we see such an improvement in the kids. They're getting healthier and stronger," Cunningham says.

The Cunninghams have tapped their own savings—and those of their patrons—and rallied thousands of Colorado high schoolers to give back to Ethiopia. Tammy and friend Betsy Wiersma, both beaders, also created the HOPE bracelet project. Beaders from across the United States donate specialty and sterling silver beads, which are made into limited-edition HOPE bracelets. More than $200,000 in bracelet proceeds have streamed back to Yetebon. Project Mercy is run by Ethiopia's first woman senator, Marta Gabre-Tsadick, and her husband, Demeke.

The Cunninghams now have their own foundation, the Cunningham Foundation (www.cunninghamfoundation.org), and a new dream: high-school students everywhere participating in a new give-back venture called Quarters for Kids, in which students pool their quarters to help Ethiopian kids. "A quarter buys breakfast. A quarter buys lunch," says Cunningham. "We have a responsibility to show teens this is a road they can go down. They can feel good, have fun, and make a difference." The Cunninghams often bring high-school kids along on their visits to Ethiopia.

Members of the swelling "giving while living" crowd, the Cunninghams believe in gifting their favorite causes while they're still around to enjoy it. They also throw their philanthropic weight behind lots of Colorado give-back projects, including homeless shelters and kids' food programs. On Mother's Day, they close their restaurant to the public and instead fete elderly women who've nowhere else to go. "How cool is that? We see them eating brunch and feeling the love of volunteers. I can't enjoy that when I'm dead," Cunningham says.

They may be helping African kids find their place in the world, say the Cunninghams, sitting in their light-filled, elegant restaurant, the snowcapped Rockies in the distance, as diners tuck into plates of blackened swordfish. But they've found their place, as well. "I've gone from being a shopaholic to a workaholic to do what I can for people who can't do for themselves. More shoes don't matter. More clothes don't matter. This matters," Tammy says.

Ordinary Oprahs on the Move

As Oprah opened her long-dreamed-of academy in South Africa in 2007, millions of us felt the love. Not just because it was a gorgeous facility on fifty-two beautiful acres. Not just because the state-of-the-art libraries and theaters shone. But because we connected with that breakout joy streaming off the young girls as they stepped inside their school—and into their future. When Oprah said, "When you educate a girl, you begin to change the face of a nation," you could almost hear the collective cheers going up around the world.

We get it that education is a sure pathway to peace, prosperity, and more stability around the globe. We really get that. We just aren't always sure what to do to help make that happen. But if you look closely among your neighbors and friends and throughout your community, you'll pretty quickly find ordinary Oprahs, like the Cunninghams, putting up schools, stocking libraries, and making sure kids hungry to learn aren't just standing outside the schoolyards peering in.

Most of the time, these ordinary Oprahs are toiling alongside hardworking local villagers willing to carry supplies for miles just to bring a school to their piece of the world.

"I've seen mothers carrying cement bags over steep mountain slopes to build a school no one thought possible. I've seen parents come together to dig foundations. People are not afraid of hard work," says John Wood, founder of Room to Read, which promotes literacy in Nepal, India, Sri Lanka, Cambodia, Laos, Vietnam, and Africa.

Do What You Love with What You've Got

Is education a give-back window you may want to step through? Do you feel called to help the world's kids become all they can be? Would you find it big fun to help kids read their first book?

If so, there's an explosion of organizations doing everything from putting up schools and libraries to tutoring English to delivering solar power to villages with no electricity so children can stay up at night and read. Whether you personally roll up your sleeves and help build a school or library from the ground up, or build a school community from afar with your goodwill, it's bound to be the education of *your* lifetime as well.

But don't choose this kind of volunteering out of pity or the need to fix someone, because the people you'll meet or serve aren't broken or in need of a quick fix. They aren't looking for your pity; they're looking for an education that will lead to employment.

Do this kind of volunteering because it makes your heart grow three sizes larger when you connect with and help other human beings. Do it because it makes *you* more human. As the Cunninghams say, "Do what you love. Do what you are able. Do it from your heart."

Here's Your Challenge: At Least 120 Million School-Aged Children Aren't Getting an Education

That's because of a lack of school fees, buildings, teachers, supplies—or of a safe, war-free environment in which to study. Living in fierce poverty, some are forced at early ages into child labor, sex trafficking, or other high-risk situations. Girls are still denied an education, because cultural beliefs favor schooling for boys only.

One in five people can't begin to read this paragraph: that's 850 million illiterate people—two-thirds of whom are women—according to Room to Read (www.roomtoread.org).

ONE TARGET TO SHOOT FOR

World leaders gathered in 2000 and set the UN Millennium Development Goals. One of the goals: aim to provide primary education for all children by 2015. That's six years away.

If enough of us make a difference, we can draw closer to that goal.

What could we do to make those Millennium Development Goals more than just words on a document? And how might it change your life if you changed the life of a child with the appetite to learn? What would it be like to help a child become the next Oprah, the next five-star restaurant owner, the next doctor, store owner, teacher, or engineer?

Here are some entry points, beginning with ways you can travel and help put up schools and libraries.

Here's Your Opportunity

HELP PUT UP SCHOOLS AND LIBRARIES

If you really want to rally around this issue, here's a sampling of volunteer-vacation opportunities that would welcome your passion:

🐑 **Globe Aware:** Volunteer in Ghana in the capital of the Volta Region, Ho, in southeast Ghana, near Mount Adaklu. Beautiful, lush landscapes and diverse ecology contrast with the lack of teachers or educational facilities. Volunteers help build school structures, desks, and blackboards, mix mud for bricks, or paint classrooms in villages outside of Ho. "Volunteers are very cherished!" says Catherine McMillan, Globe Aware rep. "The chief of each village makes a big deal about greeting volunteers, and they put together times to teach volunteers local dances." You can also construct chalkboards, build desks, and do basic repairs at schools in Laos, Vietnam, Thailand, China, Romania, and Cambodia. Consider that your jobs may vary widely. In Laos, you may also go to a nearby orphanage and do projects like assembling a rabbit cage. This may seem like a trivial thing, but it's not, McMillan says. Children often have limited access to protein. The orphanage has asked for help constructing rabbit cages so the rabbits can be a source of protein for their children.

Then you may also practice English with the children, paint walls, repair roofs, help build a ball court, or help children create puppets for a puppet show. www.globeaware.org

ProWorld: ProWorld has opportunities to build schools in Peru, Belize, Mexico, India, and Thailand. www.myproworld.org

Global Volunteers: Help construct and repair classrooms in India. In Ecuador, help landscape, paint, and upgrade a new day-care/school facility in Calderon, on the outskirts of Quito. At Camp Hope in Quito, you can support the ongoing repair of classrooms and playgrounds. www.globalvolunteers.org

Needs Can Shift Overnight in the Developing World

You may go to a school project and assume you'll only be building classroom desks, teaching English, or painting walls. But keep in mind that the needs in your community can shift drastically, depending on the conditions, and you want to be flexible enough to respond.

Take its Vietnamese project, says Globe Aware's McMillan: "We generally focus on teaching English and the mobile library project, but recently there was much flooding in Vietnam, so the last group was utilized to go and deliver food supplies to needy communities. During this program, the itinerary changed based on the greatest current need."

❧ **Volunteer Nepal:** Volunteer Nepal invites volunteers to help install windows, repair doors, build bookshelves, and help with other school construction and maintenance projects. www.volunteernepal.org

❧ **Village Volunteers:** Put in an organic garden for a school; build a playground, library, school, or preschool; or help in a school in a rural village in Kenya, Ghana, India, or Nepal. Village Volunteers customizes international volunteer opportunities for students, professionals, retirees, families, and small groups and encourages volunteers to share their own special talents. For instance, volunteers may also support local research projects, or work with traditional healers, musicians, or artisans, or document oral accounts to capture and preserve cultural and family history for orphans. www.villagevolunteers.org

❧ **Peacework:** Help build schools in Vietnam, where Peacework has constructed about twenty schools since 1997. All the projects are conducted with local village leadership and volunteers, so each project is a mix of people, cultures, and resources. www.peacework.org

❧ **Building with Books:** Building with Books reaches out to U.S. students not involved in after-school programs and helps them build schools in Haiti, Nepal, Nicaragua, Malawi, Mali, and Senegal. www.buildingwithbooks.org

❧ **Greenforce:** You can help build and support mountain schools in Nepal—and later visit an elephant-breeding center, trek rhinos and Bengal tigers, and raft on rivers swollen with Himalayan runoff. www.greenforce.org

&o **Volunteer Africa:** Work alongside villagers in Tanzania, building projects they've initiated themselves, such as village dispensaries, school classrooms, pit latrines, and staff houses for teachers and medical staff. www.volunteerafrica.org

&o **Amizade:** Help construct the first public library outside the capital city in Ghana. www.amizade.org

&o **Global Citizens Network:** Help expand and renovate classrooms in Tanzania. www.globalcitizens.org

QUESTIONS TO ASK

- What skills will I need?
- How much manual labor is involved?
- Will I be carrying trusses or roofing material—or painting school bathrooms?
- And if I can't carry heavy bricks or equipment, what else can I do?
- Will I be working with local people?
- Is the school/library affiliated with any particular religious or political organization?
- Is there a particular curriculum or educational program you're spreading?
- What will happen when we go home?
- Who'll attend this school?
- Who will maintain it so it's not abandoned?

If you grab your hammer and go overseas to put up a classroom, you'll also became a global student yourself, getting a rare chance to grow and evolve as a real part of the worldwide community.

Here's how San Francisco student Jonathan Orc describes his transformation as he helped build a school in Mali in 2007 through Building with Books.

One Volunteer's Journey: One of the Most Memorable Experiences in My Life

I guess you could say it was a real turning point. I joined Building with Books three years ago, because I had nothing to do with my life and I was getting bored. Before that, I was quiet and always had a lot of doubts about myself—only alcohol and drugs made me feel better. I didn't have any friends that I could talk to about how I felt. My relationship with my family was not good, because they didn't trust me.

When the day came for me to leave for Africa, I wasn't really excited to go there. I was upset that I would miss my spring break and worried that I'd miss my friends. At first, I thought this trip was going to suck and that I wouldn't make friends.

I thought Africa would be a very bad place: very hot, very poor, full of sickness and dirt—just like what you see on TV. Because the only way to see what's going on around the world is the media—they're like the eyes of the world.

There were like fifteen of us, including students and teachers, who traveled from San Francisco to Africa. When I arrived in Mali, I was shocked at how hot it was. Right away I thought, "This is nothing like the United States."

We barely saw any cars on the roads. Most people walk or ride motorcycles. The roads are really dusty and the whole country smells different. Not bad, just different. We took a jeep to the village of Don Kelena, which was really isolated. It was away from any hospitals or markets. At first, I felt like, "What the hell am I doing here?"

But even though Africa's really poor, the thing that is better than the United States is the people. When we arrived in Don Kelena, all the people out there accepted us like we were one of them. They offered us their homes and their support for helping them. I felt accepted as soon as I stepped off the jeep.

We arrived at night, but they had been waiting for us all day long. It was weird, but I didn't feel different from them. I felt that I belonged there, like they were just saving a spot for me in their village the whole time. I never really thought that they would spread their arms and accept us as family and not just as guests.

On my first night, I was reading a translation book of their language—called Bambara—while they were setting up their huts for us. I was looking for the words to say "thank you," and a whole bunch of people from the village started reading the book with me: the old people, the kids, the teenagers. I taught them how to speak English, and they taught me how to speak their language.

I Had Never Felt So Good about Myself Before

I was so proud of myself. I never really thought that I could teach other people and learn from them at the same time. It was priceless. And the very next day, everybody started following me around and giving me more respect and starting to accept me more as one of them.

I met a lot of cool people out there, like a rapper, a doctor, a fortune teller, and guys who had three wives. There were kids who always gave me mangoes and followed me around to help me with everything, even if I didn't need their help.

Building a schoolhouse out there was really hard, because it was all manual. You have to do it yourself, because they don't have any machines. You have to mix the cement, make bricks, dig ten feet down and flatten the ground, and carry bricks. Even though I was the one who had the most experience in construction work of the group, even I looked like a beginner at this work. But even though we were not as good as the people in the village, they still let us do it, because they wanted us to experience how hard the work is and how fun it is at the same time.

I didn't miss anything from the United States at all while

I was there, not even my family—probably because I was having so much fun out there. I think it was a new beginning for me, because I felt different after I came home.

Leaving there was a really hard thing to do. I had only been there for a week, but I felt like I was there forever. I have never felt so welcomed, so accepted, and so proud of what I've done. It made me realize that any place can be beautiful, even though the people there don't have much money, big houses, or nice clothes. We don't need those things. We don't need to value material things.

What we need to realize is that there's more out there. You just have to open your eyes. Going in there and experiencing what's out there opened my eyes, and what we all need is each other.

All the things that I used to think about—like clothes, shoes, cell phones, and iPods—changed. All the things I used to think were cool didn't look that cool to me anymore. All of a sudden, I valued experiences more than material things. I talk more; I have fun more often; and I feel happier.

Before, I used to see Africa as a crappy place, but now I see it at as a paradise, because here you don't see stars in the sky at night; you don't see the moon shine on you; you don't see the clouds make weird shapes; and you don't see real smiles from people. Africa is a beautiful and extraordinary place that changed my life.

TEACH ENGLISH TO EAGER STUDENTS

If working with your hands doesn't appeal to you, consider teaching English abroad. There are seemingly endless volunteer-vacation organizations to teach English, in places ranging from Ecuador to Hungary. Here's a sampling:

❧ **Global Volunteers:** Global Volunteers has opportunities to tutor young AIDS orphans outside Malengeni, a small agricultural village in South Africa. Global Volunteers also has opportunities to teach conversational English skills in Brazil, China, the Cook Islands, Ecuador, Ghana, Greece, Hungary, India, Mexico, Peru, Romania, South Africa, Tanzania, and other countries. Some extended-stay options are available for up to forty weeks. www.globalvolunteers.org

❧ **Global Volunteer Network:** Teach English in rural China, Vietnam, Cambodia, Nepal, India, and other countries. A new program in South Africa allows volunteers to be teaching assistants and tutors in primary and secondary schools in South Africa. www.volunteer.org.nz

❧ **WorldTeach:** WorldTeach offers short-term and long-term teaching opportunities in Chile, China, Cost Rica, Ecuador, Rwanda, the Marshall Islands, Namibia, and many other countries. Most volunteers live with host families or on the school campus, so you have a chance to really immerse yourself in the local culture (see sidebar). www.worldteach.org

ℝ **Projects Abroad:** Projects Abroad has opportunities to teach English in twenty-two different countries, from Bolivia to Romania to Senegal. www.projects-abroad.org

ℝ **World Endeavors:** Teach English in countries including Costa Rica, Ecuador, Brazil, Thailand, the Philippines, India, Nepal, and Ghana. www.worldendeavors.org

So Much More than English Teachers: WorldTeach

WorldTeach is an opportunity not just to teach English abroad, but also to nurture your global citizenship and promote international development and understanding of other cultures, says Helen Claire Sievers, WorldTeach executive director: "Face-to-face connections...meeting real people in real life, helps volunteers transform all preconceived ideas."

Like many of the volunteer organizations, WorldTeach is growing rapidly. It's been sending volunteer teachers into the developing world since 1985. Six years ago, about 125 teacher volunteers went abroad. Now about 400 are going each year. "People are recognizing the world is increasingly global, and if they want to play a part in that, it's necessary to know more," says Sievers.

WorldTeach's opportunities, especially the yearlong placements, heighten volunteers' international awareness and understanding of poverty, diseases, illiteracy, and other conditions, making it no longer possible to live in a cocoon, she says. "You see suffering and the lack of resources, not just of money but of intellectual capacity and opportunities. When you see that, how can you go home and just play tennis?"

Sievers speaks from personal experience as well. She spent eighteen years living in the Marshall Islands, where she was a high-school principal, a hospital administrator, community court judge, and director of a handicraft co-op. She joined WorldTeach in 2001.

WorldTeach got its start in 1985 and has placed thousands of volunteers throughout Africa, Eastern Europe, Latin America, Asia, and the Pacific Islands. The organization has seven- to eight-week summer programs and yearlong programs as well. It sends teacher volunteers to Bangladesh, Chile, Ecuador, Kenya, Mongolia, Rwanda, China, Namibia, South Africa, and other countries.

You don't have to be a classroom teacher or have classroom teaching experience, but WorldTeach is looking for candidates with a "demonstrated interest in and commitment to teaching," its site says. Some volunteers may teach subjects as varied as computer skills or empowerment. The large majority simply want to do something really different and want to do something meaningful, Sievers says.

"Our WorldTeach volunteers have done amazing things both in- and outside the classroom," she says. "Most are involved somehow in making their schools or their communities better. We had a volunteer in the remote Amerindian region of Guyana who directed a play that ran at the national theater. We had a volunteer in Costa Rica who, with his class, built a basketball court. They hauled sand from the river to make the cement and got the local carver to make the backboard.

"We had a volunteer in Ecuador who raised over $10,000 for scholarships so local students could learn English at her community college. We had another in Namibia who raised enough for bed nets for all the children in her school and in the neighboring school. Many of our volunteers have built libraries, and many more have stocked libraries. Quite a few have built playgrounds for their schools."

For more info: www.worldteach.org

SHOW YOUR SKILLS

Many times, teachers are needed to present material and skills, not just teach English. Here's an example:

  Amigos de las Américas: Go to Oaxaca and help local youth learn everything from basic computing to navigating the Internet to using digital photography and video to promote and preserve their culture and document oral histories. In Paraguay, help run day camps for children, which includes helping with extracurricular activities on health and the environment, creative expression, youth leadership, and team building. Past volunteers have focused on teaching everything from nutrition to cultural exchange to dental hygiene. www.amigoslink.org

Teaching in other countries not only gives you a chance to take a personal bite out of illiteracy; it also allows you to see a culture up close and personal.

Helping Out from Home: Find an Organization with a Global Reach

Check out the following education-focused organizations that reach out around the globe from right here at home. Speak to their staff, and see if they might be a match for your interests.

Room to Read: Used to setting the world on fire with software solutions, Microsoft executive John Wood took a soul-searching trip to the Himalayas. He was shocked to discover a Nepalese village where the kids had few books, save a tourist's cast-off Danielle Steeles. Wood began to burn with a different desire. He sent an email request to his friends and family asking for book donations, and they poured into his parents' garage.

Wood bundled thousands of books on the back of a yak and put up a six-hundred-student school on one of the highest peaks in the Himalayas—for starters. Now Wood is the founder and director of Room to Read, which he says is bent on completing "the biggest educational build out in the developing world...We open four libraries a day and two schools each week somewhere in the developing world. We have to go big on this. We are not supposed to think small."

Room to Read currently operates in Cambodia, India, Laos, Nepal, Sri Lanka, and Vietnam and is now building in South

Africa. Participating communities invest in their own schools and libraries by raising a portion of the project funds through donated land, labor, materials, or cash.

Wood is now hooked on giving back. "Imagine row after row of children lining up with marigold garlands, saying *namasté* over and over," Wood says, remembering one of his school visits. "My parents always said, 'What you make doesn't make you a good person. What you do with what you make makes you a good person.' That's why I had to leave Microsoft. It was getting in my way of getting copies of *Go Dog Go* into kids' hands."

Results: Room to Read has impacted the lives of over 1.3 million children by...

- constructing 287 schools
- establishing over 3,870 libraries
- publishing 146 new local language children's titles, representing over 1.3 million books
- donating over 1.4 million English language children's books
- funding 3,448 long-term scholarships for girls
- establishing 136 computer and language labs

Check out all the many ways to support Room to Read on its site, including (1) introducing Room to Read to your employer or another possible corporate sponsor; (2) joining or starting a Room to Read chapter in your area; or (3) conducting a book drive in your school or workplace. Download Room to Read's Book Drive Kit to find out more. www.roomtoread.org

>
> "We need to prove to the rest of the world that Americans are generous."
>
> *—John Wood,*
> *Room to Read*

Central Asia Institute: Aziza, who lives along the Afghan border of Pakistan, longed to be the first girl to go to school in her valley of four thousand people. But boys often threw stones at her or stole her books to hold her back. With the support of Central Asia Institute (CAI), Aziza studied pre- and postnatal care. Her dream: stop the number of women dying in childbirth. Aziza now earns one dollar a day as a maternal-care worker—and she hasn't lost one woman in childbirth since 2000.

Greg Mortenson's world was also shaken up when he stumbled into a poor Pakistani village after a perilous, failed descent down K2 in 1993. As he regained his strength, Mortenson was appalled to see the village had no school. He vowed to come back and rebuild one.

He founded CAI, which, since 1996, has boosted literacy and education, especially for girls, in Afghanistan and Pakistan. It has built sixty-one schools in the region for about twenty-two thousand students. Amazingly, each school only costs about $20,000.

An arm of CAI is Pennies for Peace, which helps support CAI, one penny at a time. Since its 1995 beginning as Pennies for Pakistan, Pennies for Peace has raised more than seventeen million pennies.

Remember six-year-old Morgan Atwell, who pooled her pennies to help kids in Afghanistan and Pakistan? She's one of Pennies for Peace's allies, raising more than $700 for the organization. "Kids have a natural desire to help," says Pennies for Peace director Christiane Leitinger. "We want to help them access that place where they know they can change the world."

The Taliban continues to bomb or shut down schools in Pakistan. The devastating earthquake in 2005 destroyed 9,200 schools. CAI estimates that Pakistan needs from 12,000 to 15,000 new schools; Afghanistan, 3,500.

Read more about Greg Mortenson's mission in his book, *Three Cups of Tea,* and visit his website for ideas, events, and suggestions of ways to donate. www.threecupsoftea.com

Free the Children: This organization has put up more than five hundred schools around the world with the help of one million young people in the United States—and has helped one million youth in this country connect with the rest of the world. When you adopt a village, you can help put up schools and health centers and support alternative income projects in Kenya, Sierra Leone, China, and Sri Lanka. You also can send school and health kits, with items ranging from toothbrushes to notebooks and pencils. www.freethechildren.org

World Neighbors: This group also lets you adopt a village with a donation of $2,500 a year or more. When you do so, you receive a profile of the village each year to show what impact your donation has. www.wn.org

Teachers Without Borders: Imagine classrooms with no desks, so students use one another's backs for writing. This is just one reality developing-world teachers face. Teachers Without Borders offers curriculum, training, and support for teachers struggling to educate kids with little resources. By using innovative technology and gathering the best collective wisdom from teachers in every culture, TWB focuses on building teacher leaders in the developing world, in everything from computer skills to science. TWB founder Fred Mednick says, "When you work on education, you work on water, HIV/AIDS, human rights. We have worked with Pakistani women to ensure that they have clean water and education and with Nigerians to incorporate HIV/AIDS education into teacher training. We've opened schools in refugee camps that also provide health education for paraprofessionals." www.teacherswithoutborders.org

> "You can hand out condoms, build roads, put in electricity, but nothing will change until the girls are educated. They are the ones who remain at home. They are the ones who instill the values. Educating the girls is a long-term solution to the war on poverty, and that will have a big impact on the war on terrorism."
>
> —Greg Mortenson,
> *Central Asia Institute director.*

MY ENCOUNTER WITH A GIRL HUNGRY TO LEARN

As I walked through the slums of Kampala, Uganda, past women squatting in the red soil to wash out metal bowls or tend a fire as they cobbled together a meal, I suddenly felt a strange tingling sensation on the back of my head. I swiveled around and saw a little girl following me and my traveling companion, Connie Regan-Blake, a mesmerizing storyteller. Connie and I were gathering stories from the beaders of BeadforLife and about to duck into a small hut for our first visit of the day when the little girl rushed to my side.

She insisted—firmly—on carrying my camera tripod. She flashed a shy smile and seemed considerably bolder than other kids who were peering out at the *muzunga* (white people) from behind their mothers' skirts.

She pointed to a small bag of hickory nuts that my parents had sent, which I was carrying for a midday snack. When I saw her distended belly, I knew she was likely starving, like the thousands of people radiating around us on that hillside suspended above Kampala. I gave the nuts to her and watched as she delicately pulled out just a few and chewed them slowly like they were expensive truffles. What I would have tossed down for a quick boost was possibly her sustenance for a long time.

"What's your name?" I asked. "Mildred," she said softly, clutching my tripod tighter. Mildred continued to follow us through a warren of homes and families, many sitting outdoors, too many unemployed, too much time to pass idly, too few kids in school.

Just as Connie and I were about to duck into another home for a visit, Mildred made her move. She grabbed my left hand and tugged hard, forcing me to look down at her. "I want to go to school," she said, her brown eyes smiling but intense, too intense for a little girl.

Oh, my god. My stomach lurched. What to say now to this precious child that didn't sound lame or meaningless? I didn't want to promise something I couldn't begin to deliver. A horrible pocket of silence hung between us as she held onto my hand. And drilled deeper into my heart with her eyes. So I said the only thing that felt right, knowing still that it likely sounded as empty as her stomach.

"Honey, I *do* hope you get to go to school someday. I hope you do." Mighty Mildred wasn't about to let me off the hook that easily. She pulled on my hand again, harder this time, and I felt it pulse up my shoulder. Then she leaned in and placed her hand gently on my stomach, as if sensing the turmoil in my gut. "I—want—to—go—to—school," Mildred reiterated. Again I said, "Honey, I *do* hope you get to go to school."

When I got home, I did more homework to better understand Mildred's world. Finding places for millions of the Mildreds hungry to go to school is, according to a December 30, 2006, *New York Times* article, one of sub-Saharan Africa's "most overwhelming and gratifying missions. After two decades of sluggish growth in enrollment rates, the region's forty-five countries find themselves with an embarrassment of eager schoolchildren."

Almost twenty-two million more African students flooded classrooms between 1999 and 2004, boosting the enrollment rate by 18 percent. Many parents are embracing education as never before, because they see a different future for their children and want to move their country in a new direction.

But textbooks, literacy, and school buildings are all in such short supply across the continent. AIDS is killing teachers faster than countries can train them. I now knew I wanted to pay for Mildred's school fees, and I had a few friends, like my friend Cindy, who were eager to do so, too. But instead of helping educate Mildred, I got a further education in the ways of the developing world. Despite contacting numerous nonprofits, I was not able to find a trustworthy sponsoring organization working in her area of Kampala that could guarantee it could enroll Mildred. So she continues to call to me and serve as my reminder that there aren't always neat, tidy endings in the developing world. Not yet, anyway.

DISCOVER THE GROUPS THAT REACH OUT FROM YOUR NECK OF THE WOODS

Look around. There's bound to be an organization right in your own community tackling education issues in the developing world. Start by narrowing down the type of organization you want to work with. Do you want to support African refugees struggling to get an education here? This appealed to me. What about putting up a school or library in another country? Visit your local and regional newspaper websites, and see if there's a match. Use Google. Talk with local librarians, university centers, school principals, churches, and volunteer clearinghouses. Visit with them, and see what you might do. When I looked more closely, this is what I found in Denver, one hour away:

✺ **Project Education Sudan:** "Education is more important to us than food." When Carol Francis-Rinehart heard those words from the young African men around her, she realized she couldn't just drop off her food donation and go. She'd come to visit briefly with a cluster of Lost Boys from Sudan, intending to leave behind some groceries and a bicycle and return home. The Lost Boys of Sudan are more than twenty-seven thousand boys, now young men, who were displaced and forced to flee Sudan when civil war broke out beginning in the early 1980s. In 2001, about 3,800 Lost Boys were resettled throughout the United States.

Rinehart now helps the Lost Boys return and rebuild the home-land they fled more than twenty years ago when war broke out, shattering their childhoods. Rinehart and former Lost Boy Isaac Khor Bher head Project Education Sudan, which helps the young men reunite with family and rebuild schools for about fifty-one thousand southern Sudanese who live with no electricity, running water, or health care.

In 2005, Rinehart and Khor Bher slammed down on Sudan's scarred red soil in a bush plane swollen with kilos of rice, beans, onions, salt, water, and cooking oil. Sidestepping land mines, they drove through the countryside to finally reach Isaac's village. Few things looked familiar to Isaac, but his mother recognized him. She'd been leaving her thatch-roofed *tukel* for a month to wait outside for her son. She ran to Isaac in a driving rain, considered a blessing and good omen in the Dinka tribal culture, and folded her son into her arms singing the lullaby she sang to him as a child: "You are very strong, my very strong lion."

Tribespeople sang, danced, cheered, and slaughtered goats in their honor. After hours of meeting under the hot, 115-degree shade of the thau tree, the elders and chiefs decided they would like to bring education to the girls of their village. Rinehart and Khor Bher went back home to Denver and founded Project Education Sudan (PES). They returned the following year with a team of ten, including three Lost Boys. They drilled two water wells, delivered three grinding mills to emancipate the girls from hours of laborious hand grain grinding, taught accounting to school and clergy, and reunited the three Lost Boys with their families.

The outcome of the elders meeting in Isaac's village of Konbek resulted in PES starting an all-girls boarding school.

Lost Boy Lual Awok installed solar electricity in a primary school in his village of Maar, making it a first-ever power hub for miles around. "The people of Maar stayed up all night with the lights on in the school drumming, singing, and dancing in gratitude for the first electric light they had ever experienced. They were so proud of their returning hero, Lost Boy Lual Aowk," Rinehart remembers.

It's a testament to the young men like Awok and Khor Bher that they've somehow managed to hang onto their deep love of country— when they could barely hold on to life at times in their odyssey.

Khor Bher remembers sitting by the fire as his grandfather told stories of their ancestors while bullfrogs sang to the inky African night. He thinks he was about seven. Sometimes he'd be lulled to sleep in the light by his grandfather's voice. But the firelight turned ugly when civil war erupted in Isaac's village. He and tens of thousands of young boys fled, barefoot, and became a swollen river of misery, typically moving under the cover of night, attacked by marauding hyenas and lions. "I'd hear every footstep the animal took and feel the air as it jumped next to me. I'd hear boys screaming and animals tearing them apart," Khor Bher says.

Now the tall, long-limbed man, whose name "Khor" means "lion," is increasingly hearing the sound of hope for his people: "I hope that telling my story over and over will bring awareness and hurry the help."

About 3,600 former Lost Boys, many of whom have gone on to receive good educations, now live in the United States. Project

Education Sudan provides the Lost Boys/Girls of Sudan the opportunity to give back to their homeland by advising and working together with Americans to build hope through building schools and providing equal education to all in the most rural areas of southern Sudan. www.projecteducationsudan.org

SET UP A SCHOOL CULTURAL EXCHANGE

Help kids discover how much they have in common with kids around the world. Set up or advocate for a cultural exchange in a classroom near you. If we fell more in love with one another's art, music, storytelling, and culture, think of how harmonious the world would become.

Here are a couple of cool groups making those connections:

One World Youth Project: A unique sister-school program for middle- and high-school students, OWYP links schools and youth groups around the world in learning partnerships for cultural exchange and collaborative community service toward the achievement of the UN Millennium Development Goals. OWYP was founded by eighteen-year-old Jessica Rimington and is entirely managed and operated by volunteers. www.oneworldyouthproject.org

OneWorld Classrooms: If you can't take your class abroad, here's the next best thing to get to know our neighbors around the world. This organization has coordinated cultural exchanges between more than five hundred classrooms worldwide. The majority of these exchanges involve schools in the developing world. For instance, students in New York and Pennsylvania are getting to know Ecuadorian students on the edge of the Amazon, where the rain forest intersects the Andes Mountains. The students are exchanging writing, art, video, maps, and emails to get a sense of each other's world. This is just one cultural exchange underway; see what you can do. In many cases, U.S. partner classes have raised money or contributed school materials for their overseas partners. www.oneworldclassrooms.org

Helping in the United States: Improve Educational Opportunities Here

If you want to help kids here get a better education and make their way in the world, here are a few great opportunities:

🐝 **Global Volunteers:** Global Volunteers offers volunteer programs in Minnesota, Montana, and West Virginia. In Minnesota, you can tutor children of new immigrants who've streamed in from various countries, such as Guatemala, Russia, Somalia, Cambodia, and Ethiopia. This project focuses on teaching English to help immigrants transition into the United States, but no teaching experience is necessary. In Montana, you can serve the youth and adults of the Blackfoot Nation by constructing and repairing playgrounds, supporting education projects, and working on other assignments. In West Virginia, you can find opportunities to tutor youth in the historic coal-mining towns of Appalachia, where high poverty levels and limited employment opportunities are ongoing challenges. www.globalvolunteers.org

❦ **ProLiteracy Worldwide:** Volunteer to teach English, math, writing, or job-interviewing, computer, and other skills with this established organization. www.literacyvolunteers.org

❦ **Amizade:** Help tutor and mentor youth of the Navajo Nation in Tuba City, Arizona. You can also help in the computer labs, libraries, and reading rooms, as well as with physical education. www.amizade.org

❦ **Experience Corps:** If you're over fifty-five, become a tutor or mentor for an elementary-school student struggling to learn to read through this award-winning intergenerational program. Experience Corps is in nineteen cities across the United States, from New York City to Portland, Oregon. www.experiencecorps.org

❦ **City Year:** This spectacular organization unites young people who serve for a full year as tutors, mentors, and role models for kids in schools and neighborhoods across the United States and South Africa. City Year is now in eighteen locations, from Boston and Detroit to Little Rock and Los Angeles. You can plan and lead after-school and vacation programs or service-learning projects, or teach health, public safety, and other activities. www.cityyear.org

❦ **Year Up:** This one-year, intensive training program provides urban young adults with technical and professional skills, college credits, an education stipend, and corporate apprenticeships at one of more than seventy leading companies, from Bank of America to Merrill Lynch. Your volunteer skills and support are needed to help kids learn job-preparation, leadership, interviewing, computer, and other skills. Year Up operates in Providence, New York City, Boston, San Francisco, and Washington, D.C., and hopes to ultimately serve tens of thousands of urban adults around the country. www.yearup.org

Citizen Schools: Volunteer to share your skills as a Citizen Teacher at schools in New Jersey, Massachusetts, New York, North Carolina, Texas, New Mexico, or California. Since 1995, this organization has brought thousands of citizens into middle schools to help kids learn real-world skills. www. citizenschools.org

Icouldbe: Explore this great virtual-volunteering opportunity. Become a volunteer career mentor, and help a student successfully transition from college to career. This organization's nationally recruited e-mentors have helped more than four thousand at-risk teens. www.icouldbe.org

Teach for America: This is the national corps of college graduates who commit two years to teach in urban and rural public schools. More than six thousand corps members teach in twenty-nine urban and rural regions around the country. Consider sending a donation to Teach for America, which has more than fourteen thousand alumni—now in their twenties and thirties— many of whom are assuming leadership roles in educational and social reform. www.teachforamerica.org

⌘ **Backpack Club:** See if your community has a Backpack Club, which can use donations of food, school supplies, and other items for kids living in poverty or challenging situations. Some are managed by community food banks, schools, universities, and local volunteers. Stacey Sheppard started her London, Kentucky, Backpack Club, which sends about 1,450 kids per week home with backpacks brimming with everything from soup and crackers to granola bars. www.thebackpackclub.org

CHAPTER FIVE

Global Health

Deliver Clean Water to Villages, Prevent AIDS, Ease Orphans' Suffering

"The globe is so much smaller now. An ocean away, there's a girl who fell asleep holding my hand."

—Janice Green,
who worked in a Thai orphanage for part
of her volunteer vacation

We love epic stories in which achievements overcome adversity and hope transforms desperation. These stories are our North Star, our confirmation that all's well in the world.

Many such stories light the earth right now, as legions, from global health pioneers to newbie volunteers, go head-to-head with AIDS, malaria, polluted water, and other global health challenges.

Is it because Bill and Melinda Gates are investing half of their tremendous wealth in everything from finding a vaccine for malaria to making it easier to access lifesaving AIDS medicines? Or is it because we just plain feel the urgency to rise up and act and exercise our power to make a difference, knowing that from sunrise to sundown, millions are dying from preventable conditions?

For whatever reason, ordinary volunteers are setting in motion an unprecedented rollout of antiretroviral medications, immunizations, clean water systems, anti-malaria bed nets, and other aid.

Blinders are coming off; awareness is exploding; and everyday activists are responding as our world collides with the world where six million people still die of tuberculosis, malaria, and AIDS each year, and 1.2 billion people still live on less than one dollar a day. What could be your piece of this?

Big Thinking—Bold Actions

People are thinking big, really big, and daring us to go there, too. This "possibility thinking" is shifting the world community and consciousness to a more humane place. Just one example: When Bill Clinton launched his HIV/AIDS initiative in 2002, only 135,000 people in the developing world were able to access the antiretroviral medicines (ARVs) that could save their lives. The cost of the lifesaving ARVs was just too high for many people. The Clinton Foundation says that, today, 2.5 million people in the developing world receive ARV treatment, and over 750,000 of them are receiving lower cost ARV medicines purchased under agreements forged by the foundation. "Private citizens have more opportunity to do good than at any time in American history," Clinton says.

I find this as exciting as anything I've experienced in my lifetime. The ways you and I can be part of this massively hopeful effort are rising daily, literally. A humanitarian tipping point has begun, and the passion for global health has never been higher, hotter, or more ripe for engagement.

One Volunteer's Journey: Deep in a Ghanaian Village

Amanda Anderson-Green was drawn to volunteering in Ghana through a Cross-Cultural Solutions trip, because "something didn't feel intuitively right about the fact that so many don't have access to basic health care. It should be a basic human right."

Anderson-Green spent three weeks in a small village, Hohoe, working in a clinic where ARV medicines, school tuition, and vouchers for paper and pencils for AIDS orphans were distributed. She found her host community amazingly generous and welcoming: "Sometimes people would put their arms around me and thank me for coming into the clinic. They said no one locally would ever step into the clinic unless they had HIV."

As ordinary Africans become more empowered in their own health care, Anderson-Green also participated in watershed exchanges. "Educational forums were held in the village center, which was outside in a clearing among the houses. It was a dedicated meeting space with wooden benches. About fifty people showed up, and some brought their own stools or stood," says Green, who wrote a report of the meetings. "The village chief came along with female healers, who were largely responsible for the health care of the people in the village, especially birthing.

"We talked with villagers about their basic health-care

rights and what patients have a right to demand when they go to the hospital to receive care. The people were very excited about learning more about their rights. They told us many stories about bad care or discrimination because of where they lived, their sex, religion, or financial status. They were especially concerned about the lack of confidentiality and the monetary bribes and favoritism in the hospitals. It was a dynamic conversation. I was impressed by the level of participation and passion in the community and the respect and dignity given to everyone involved. There was such a sense of 'Let's make Ghana better together.'"

Now back at her job as a research technician at Seattle Biomedical Research Institute, Anderson-Green, twenty-five, finds wonder in the people she connected with and feels more bound up in their welfare. She hopes they'll continue to advocate for their needs and get the support and infrastructure they deserve.

An African Healer's Appeal

An impassioned conversation with Eleanor, a healer who longed to help women and children, still calls to Anderson-Green: "Eleanor was quite impressive. She expressed to me her idea that the government should offer training to village healers, especially in the birthing process, to ensure better health care in the villages. She said they needed a one-room birthing center that could be kept clean and sanitary with clean water, linens, and proper utensils, along with training and supplies to help with prenatal and postnatal care. Eleanor said, 'This will help dramatically with the health of young children and their mothers.'

"She asked me, 'Can you get me the monetary help I need for this? Can you help tell others of the simple things we need?'"

After meeting Eleanor and many more people like her, Anderson-Green intends to do more global health-care advocacy. She hopes to become a doctor and says, "It's now a goal of mine to be linked with others around me and find happiness in my dependence on them. One of my favorite quotes comes from Desmond Tutu: 'Without others we are incomplete. The totally self-sufficient person is actually subhuman.' I believe that every being has something to offer the world; it's my intention to act accordingly. I want to connect with and treat people as valuable and worthy of aid and advocacy and work together for a rich success."

Whether you want to educate villagers about HIV/AIDS or deliver bed nets to give kids a fighting chance against malaria-bearing mosquitoes, our collective ability to have real traction on global health issues has never been greater. As Anderson-Green says, together we can have "rich success."

Amanda Anderson-Green traveled to Africa with the support of the Travel for Good program at Travelocity, which also tries to make volunteering overseas greener. Dan Toporek, Travelocity's vice-president for public relations, shares more about Travelocity's work in this area.

Q: *Volunteers are increasingly concerned about their carbon footprint. What is Travel for Good, and how does it ease the environmental impact of volunteering abroad?*

A: There are two pieces to this:

1) We have a program that allows any traveler to offset the carbon from their trip. All the money from this program goes to the Conservation Fund GoZero program. They have already used proceeds to plant more than twenty thousand trees in Louisiana and eastern Texas. These trees not only draw carbon from the atmosphere, but also help rebuild wildlife habitat and recreational areas.

2) We have a program called Change Ambassadors designed to help people give back and make a positive difference in the world by volunteering when they travel. The goal is to remind people that we need to travel responsibly and to give something back. People who take these trips not only help other places and people, but they create a life-changing experience for themselves. We promote these experiences on the site and allow people to apply for a $5,000 grant to take the trip. We offer two grants per quarter to consumers and one per quarter to employees.

Q: *How was Travel for Good first conceived at Travelocity?*

A: There were a few of us talking about the things that were most important to us personally, and instead of leaving the company to pursue these things, we realized we could create a program that allowed all employees to participate in something that gave even greater meaning to our jobs. We realized that it was also very complementary to Travelocity's brand promise of being the customer's champion.

Q: Why is the company strongly supporting volunteering?

A: We support both international and domestic volunteering. Not everyone can take an elaborate two-week trip, so we also want to promote volunteering in parks, rebuilding trails, etc.

Q: How do you choose your ambassadors?

A: We accept applications for our Change Ambassador grants every quarter (two for consumers and one for employees). The grants are awarded based on people's records of giving back to their community or the world through volunteering, and some need for financial assistance.

Q: Why do you think so many more people, of all ages and backgrounds, are now drawn to giving back overseas, especially in the developing world?

A: People are giving back more both here and abroad. I think the volunteering people are doing abroad reflects an increased awareness by Americans that we are part of a global economy. People see more about what's happening around the world and realize there is something they can do to help, rather than just sending a few dollars to a charity. There's nothing wrong with giving money, but people get a lot more personally by going and digging wells and teaching kids. There's no middleman.

Q: What's been the impact of Travel for Good so far?

A: Our carbon offsetting through GoZero has helped the

Conservation Fund plant more than twenty thousand trees that capture carbon and rebuild wildlife habitat and recreational areas.

The Change Ambassador program has given twenty-seven grants to amazing people and teams who are helping change the world, one trip at a time.

Here's Your Challenge: More than Forty Million People Live with HIV/AIDS

About 95 percent are in developing countries. The World Health Organization estimates that seven out of ten newly infected with HIV live in sub-Saharan Africa. And of the more than fifteen million kids who have been orphaned by AIDS, more than twelve million are in Africa, according to Partners in Health. By 2010, the number of children orphaned by AIDS is expected to be a staggering twenty-five million. At the same time, three thousand children die every day from malaria in sub-Saharan Africa. That's one child every thirty seconds. About five hundred million people a year get malaria.

Another massive global challenge? One person out of every five doesn't have clean water. Two out of every five have no access to basic sanitation. UNICEF says the lack of safe water and basic sanitation affect more than four hundred million children around the world. Each hour, two hundred children under the age of five die from drinking dirty water. "Diarrhea contracted from contaminated water is the world's second biggest killer of children under the age of five; over one million die from it every year," reports UNICEF, which puts the total annual number of cases of diarrhea among children at four billion. Plus, villagers, especially women and children, are burdened with fetching water each day, often walking miles for precious liters of water. When you're spending that much time going for water, how can you be a successful student? How can you go to work, launch a new business, or do other things to lift yourself and family out of poverty?

ONE TARGET TO SHOOT FOR

"By 2015, halt and begin to reverse the spread of HIV/AIDS and the incidence of malaria and other diseases. Halve by 2015 the proportion of people without sustainable access to safe drinking water."—The UN Millennium Development Goals, adopted by the United States and 90 other nations

Here's Your Opportunity

DISTRIBUTE MEDICINES, MALARIA NETS, CLEAN WATER, AND COMPASSION

Here's a representative sampling of volunteer trips that will allow you to dive in, roll up your sleeves, and help out on the front lines of the global health crisis. Among the opportunities: educating young people about AIDS to stop the spread of the disease, one of the developing world's best hopes for fighting the spread of HIV/AIDS. Half of the world's fifteen thousand

"Malaria is equivalent to crashing seven jumbo jets filled with children every day."

—*Professor Wen Kilama,*
Tanzania

new infections—each day—still occurs among fifteen- to twenty-four-year-olds, according to a *New York Times* report in early 2008. The rewards of easing suffering, shining a light on health issues long invisible to the Western world, and making a difference will rock your world—and just maybe save a few lives.

❧ **Cross-Cultural Solutions:** Help improve the quality of life for young people in Tanzania through White Orange Youth, a group started by young professionals. Volunteers help educate youth on sexual health, STDs, and HIV/AIDS prevention. You may also do some fund-raising and website development and updates. In South Africa, you can help at a convalescent hospital for children who are recovering from acute medical and surgical conditions and not able to go home. Many are HIV-positive. In Costa Rica, you can help provide food, medical, and emotional support to people living with HIV/AIDS. Some are homeless and rejected by their own family members. You might teach English, help prepare and serve breakfast, sweep and mop floors, do dishes, clean windows, take residents to medical appointments, pick up medications, or purchase items from a nearby store. You'll also have opportunities to socialize with the residents, help them with lessons, and plan sports, yoga, and recreational and cultural activities. www.crossculturalsolutions.org

❧ **World Endeavors:** Travel to Ghanaian villages to teach about HIV/AIDS. Give presentations to dispel myths, teach prevention, and raise the visibility for the cause. www.worldendeavors.org

Projects Abroad: Work with the Glona Academy in Ghana, teaching people about the dangers of HIV/AIDS and STDs and encouraging them to adopt low-risk behavior. Volunteers visit schools and communities to educate the population on HIV/AIDS issues, as well as do research and evaluations of the current knowledge surrounding the issue. Or work with a center in Mexico providing professional care and counseling for people with HIV/AIDS and their families, including many terminally ill patients and HIV/AIDS orphans. In Nepal, you can provide care for and support children under ten who have HIV/AIDS. You will feed, play, and perhaps teach English and nutrition to them and counsel them on HIV/AIDS. www.projects-abroad.org

i-to-i: Work at a Kenyan orphanage for children who've lost parents to AIDS and HIV-related diseases. You will cook and serve food, assist with educational and English lessons, and possibly participate in counseling sessions. www.i-to-i.com

Global Volunteer Network: Volunteer in an AIDS hospice in India, providing patient care or home visits or researching HIV topics. www.volunteer.org.nz

Global Service Corps: Go out in Thai and Tanzanian communities, among the churches, schools, bazaars, and other forums, to raise awareness of HIV/AIDS prevention. www.globalservicecorps.org

🐚 **Volunteer Visions:** Work with orphaned children living with HIV in Thailand. Organize and play sports and games and share music, computer skills, and English lessons. In rural Ghana, you'll distribute ARV drugs, visit people at homes to provide medication and emotional support, re-enroll children who have dropped out of school due to lack of support, supply educational materials to children in school, help with vocational training of HIV-infected individuals, and other tasks. www.volunteervisions.org

🐚 **Global Volunteer Projects:** Learn how to counsel people living with HIV/AIDS and how ARV medications should be correctly used. Visit with people living with HIV/AIDS; lend your ear, and chat about their hopes, fears, and lives. Help educate people about making behavioral and lifestyle changes to prevent the transmission of HIV/AIDS, manage their health, and monitor their health and well-being. You can also spend time working with local community youth groups to help with sex education in the context of their culture. www.globalvolunteerprojects.org

🐚 **Village Volunteers:** Teach about HIV/AIDS and other public health awareness issues, help in or build a medical clinic, and explore other opportunities with this organization, which will help you customize your volunteer opportunity in rural villages in Kenya, Ghana, India, and Nepal. www.villagevolunteers.org

🐚 **ProWorld Service Corps:** If you have some basic medical training, look into this organization's health-outreach internships in Thailand. You will provide health-outreach services, such as AIDS awareness workshops, and vaccinate children. You'll get hands-on experience, working side by side with local doctors. www.myproworld.org

❧ **Global Volunteers:** Help in medical clinics in Ghana and Tanzania. You may help treat AIDS and malaria patients, many of whom have secondary infections, and support training on malaria prevention and treatment and HIV/AIDS-related issues, such as identifying the various signs and symptoms of HIV. www.globalvolunteers.org

❧ **Global Crossroad:** Join organizations working in India to foster awareness and lessen the stigma of HIV/AIDS, and to improve attitudes and behavior toward and care of HIV-infected patients. You can help provide shelter and counsel patients and their families. You'll also have a chance to train HIV-infected people to work with wood, make candles, and do tailoring so they have an opportunity to earn a living. www. globalcrossroad.com

❧ **Global Citizens Network:** Help build and support a community health-care center in Kenya. www.globalcitizens.org

Take a Different Path

If a hands-on volunteer opportunity isn't your thing, explore taking a PATH Journey to witness PATH's health work around the globe. PATH is an international nonprofit organization that improves global health and well-being. PATH currently works in more than sixty-five countries in health technologies, maternal and child health, reproductive health, vaccines and immunization, emerging and epidemic diseases, and other areas. PATH journeys are a chance to see global health problems firsthand, talk with local people, and learn how PATH programs are making a difference in the lives of people in India, Africa, and other parts of the world. For instance, in Kenya, you might visit a child-survival program in an urban slum in Nairobi, where rapid urbanization has left communities without access to basic health services. Or you might see a provincial hospital and a village's "magnet theater" performance—street theater designed to get communities talking about taboo health issues. You might also visit a PATH partner project of Ambassadors of Hope, a support-group program for people living with AIDS. Yet another day, you'll focus on PATH's work to increase women's access to family planning and reproductive health and on efforts to improve and expand care and support for people and families affected by HIV/AIDS, tuberculosis, and malaria. Then, you'll experience an HIV-prevention program in a local school and visit a SafeT Stop, a truck stop where long-haul truckers can go to take a break from the road and get information about avoiding HIV infection.

For more info: www.path.org

QUESTIONS TO ASK

- What does a typical day of volunteering look like?
- Will I help spread awareness of safe sex and HIV testing in community classes?
- Do I need to be comfortable in front of a crowd?
- If not, what can I do behind-the-scenes?
- Will I meet, feed, and bathe patients?
- Will I work in a community clinic or visit people at home to offer in-home care and counseling?
- Do I need previous medical experience?
- What level of intimacy can I expect?
- How much prejudice and stigma against people with AIDS still exists in the community/village?
- What level of intervention and care are the people now receiving?
- Will there be translators at the project, if needed?
- If I am helping with training and other community outreach seminars, how can I educate myself further about HIV/AIDS, malaria, and other issues before I leave?
- Will I be assisting any patients who are terminally ill or dying? Or assisting any births?
- Will I care for AIDS orphans?
- How can I best prepare myself, emotionally and psychologically, so I can fully be present—and enjoy the experience?
- What kind of safeguards may be needed?
- Can I talk with other volunteers and volunteer-organization staffers about their experiences, the positives and the negatives, to get a more realistic understanding of what I'll

see and face, as well as to hear how they dealt with their
emotions, from despair to hope?

This account is from Kimberly Walker, who volunteered for four
months with Global Service Corps in Tanzania.

One Volunteer's Journey: From Alarms to Rooster Awakenings

Walking off the plane on arrival in Arusha, Tanzania, I
was greeted with things I didn't expect: a mass of welcoming faces, a fragrant, almost intoxicating, air, and
absolutely no bugs! Every morning I would wake up to a
rooster announcing the day. I'd go outside for a run and
hear the nuns singing Swahili gospel hymns while they
did chores and prepared breakfast. Mornings in Tanzania
were magnificent.

Even at 6:30 a.m., the streets were filled with friendly faces, mostly uniformed children walking to school. As I'd run
by, they'd giggle and shout out, "Good morning." Some of
them would run alongside me for a short distance.

When it was time to move to my home stay, my "mama"
picked me up at the hostel with her son, Richard. We drove
to their village, which was made up of neat, small, cin-
derblock houses. People were everywhere: walking, chat-
ting, selling fruits and drinks, and the children ran freely
through the streets.

The first four weeks of my time with Global Service
Corps, I facilitated AIDS awareness lectures with

the other two volunteers. Every lecture began with introductions, opening speeches, and prayer, in the traditional African manner.

The teaching was extremely rewarding. I was able to see for myself how great the need was for accurate HIV/AIDS information. It also introduced me to one of the major contributors to the AIDS crisis in Africa: the status of women. It's frustrating to teach a group of women how to protect themselves against HIV when they don't even have the right to protect themselves against rape and sexual abuse.

Once it was time to begin my long-term project, which would last the remaining six weeks of my program, I decided to focus on women's issues. Using the various stories told to me by Tanzanian women, I wrote and produced a play about the obstacles African women face and the profound results that could be achieved by making positive choices. *Wanawake Jukwaani (Women Center Stage)* confronted the issues of sexual assault, HIV transmission, child abuse, spousal abuse, and teenage sex. I wrote the play in English, then had it translated into Swahili. Since this was my first time producing a play, I really had no idea what I was supposed to be doing; I just made it up as I went along.

The cast and crew were made up of local youth groups, women's groups, and volunteers from a local Maasai village. Not only did these men and women perform a valuable service to the community by spreading the message of empowering women, they also learned how to produce something extraordinary by working together.

Every day, my translator and I would travel to one of the groups' meeting places and rehearse the play. During rehearsals we would practice the lines and logistics of the play and, most importantly, discuss why these cultural changes were so important. This was a challenge. Being from different cultures, we didn't always see eye to eye on the issues, but we always respected each other's opinions and appreciated each other's comments.

The cast of the play ended up being over fifty people, half of whom were men. The men were constantly trying to change the play to *Wanawume Jukwaani (Men Center Stage)*. Sometimes the men would try to play the women's parts, because the women had more lines. The Maasai men even tried changing their story to make all of the women die and the men survive. I was constantly reminding everyone that the play was about women!

To promote the play, I posted flyers all over Arusha, as well as handed out invitations (in Swahili) to every woman I saw. Miraculously, *Wanawake Jukwaani* was a huge success. The day of the performance couldn't have been more amazing. There were over two hundred people in the audience. All of the performances were spectacular, and the audience participation was fantastic.

There are many lessons to be learned from the Tanzanian way of life. Tanzanians have such a sense of community.

They know all their neighbors and interact with them daily. Tanzanians conduct their lives outside. Your house is the place you sleep, but your home is the village.

Tanzania is a place where people appreciate a simple life. For many Tanzanians, there are no jobs, no medicine, no education, and little food. But they still celebrate what they have. Being exposed to that is such a gift.

Before I went to Africa, a woman asked me, "Do you really think you are going to make a difference there?" Her comment resounded in my mind. Was I going to make a difference? How can one person actually make an impact? What was I doing going to Africa anyway? Now I know how easy it is to make a difference. It's the easiest thing I've ever done.

Being a part of something bigger than myself, feeling that my actions were making a difference in the lives of people, was an extraordinary experience. The four months I spent in Tanzania were the happiest, most fulfilling months of my life. They gave me a taste of the amazing world we live in and a new and improved outlook on life.

WHEN I MET AN UNFORGETTABLE FACE OF AIDS

My teenaged son, Evan, and I were hanging out the window of the Death Railway Train as it plunged through the emerald Thai countryside, dropping down along the river Kwai. We grinned at each other, our faces pulled tight by the wind, as tamarind trees with outrageous purplish plumes, enchanting temples, and farmers tending sugarcane fields rushed past our rolling car.

Evan and I and the six other i-to-i volunteers we were traveling with soon went from swaying on train cars to bobbing like hood ornaments on elephants as our guides took us for an elephant ride in Khanchanaburi, in central Thailand. Just when I was ready to enjoy firmer ground, we were asked to take an elephant into the river and scrub it clean, which I, not a great swimmer, relished about as much as diving off the diving board in fourth grade. Midway through the elephant bath, workers on the shores suddenly called out instructions in Thai. What's this?

Ah, this is where the elephants dip us into the water. Ha ha ha. Funny Thai people. Oh, stop. Surely you're kidding, right? And this part of the tour is optional, right? This Land of Smiles is a real scream. Or is that me screaming as my elephant plunges me into water with loaf-sized dung close by? My great Thai adventure suddenly got more fertile than I wanted.

That evening at dusk, Evan and I sprawled on a houseboat with the other volunteers—Alexia, Patrick, Jen, Hazel, Claire, and Marie—as a sunset splashed the water orange and pink and distant mountains shimmered in the reflection. It was Thanksgiving back home, and our appreciation was high.

Adventuring and Giving Back in Overdrive

Other than the brief elephant dunk, this i-to-i "meaningful tour" in which we gallivanted and gave back was turning out to be better than we expected. In addition to serving meals to remote hill tribes, we'd danced, played, and served meals to gorgeous kids with AIDS, autism, and Down's syndrome. And in between, we'd swum under thundering waterfalls, shopped at amazing markets with bright saffron, green, and purple silks and bronze Buddhas, and played in the clear waters of Koh Tao, a southern island.

We'd also stuffed ourselves on awesome Thai food. It turned out that one of our guides, Tong, was a five-star chef who once worked in Los Angeles (another quirky reminder that the world's definitely getting flatter). That Thanksgiving night, we feasted by candlelight on fat, fresh red snappers and steaming vats of coconut rice soup, tart with lemongrass. As we toasted Tong and our guides and entertained ourselves with hilarious stories of Thanksgivings past, I hoped some of the joy would float out across the water, over the mountains, back up the river Kwai and somehow touch Gay, a symbol of the AIDS pandemic hitting Thailand hard.

I'd just met Gay the day before. She was a patient in an AIDS hospice opened in 1992 by a visionary monk, Alongkot Kikkapanya. The hospice was located within the Wat Phra Baat Mamphu temple in Lopburi, about 75 miles north of Bangkok. It's a refuge for people suffering with HIV/AIDS, many of whom are abandoned by their families, and it turned out to be one of my favorite moments in the whole fourteen-day adventure.

AIDS Stigmas—Abandoned Patients

The hospice still exists in too many shadows and is associated with too many stigmas. Only 10 percent of the patients' family members will show up for their cremation and the ceremony honoring their death. Meanwhile, the incidence of AIDS keeps mounting across the country.

But that urgency wasn't Father Michael Bassano's focus when we met him, moving lightly among the patients lying in white-sheeted beds along the hospice walls. We volunteers fell silent as we stepped into this holy place. But Father Mike was lively and animated, greeting us as if we were stepping into a birthday celebration, the party about to begin. "This isn't a place to die. This is a place to live," Father Mike said. "And *today*,"—he'd said the word as if it were a shining holiday, someone's birthday, a Special Day of Some Sort—"*today* some of the patients would like a massage."

Father Mike, who'd been helping the AIDS patients in Thailand for eight years, led me to Gay, a delicate woman lying in a bed at one end of the room. Gay slowly lifted one thin, long hand. If I took her outstretched palm, I sensed nothing would be quite the same. But isn't that

"AIDS statistics are numbers with the tears washed off."

—*Dr. Brigid Corrigan*

why I'd come in the first place? I wanted to go deeper in myself and in the world.

Making a Human Connection

I stepped in and started to gingerly massage Gay's palm, tentatively, awkwardly. I've never been good at massages. Just ask my husband and kids: not great massage skillage, as Evan would say. But if Gay wanted a massage, I wanted to try to honor her request.

Gay's body, I noticed, seemed thinner than the suitcase with which I'd come to her country. Her light brown limbs lay like winter branches against the snow white sheets on her bed. Her brown eyes, watching me, were wide and full.

As I stroked Gay's fingers, my mind went into overdrive. What was her world like before? What brought her to this point? Who is she, really? Where did she live? With so many on the waiting list, how did Gay manage to make it to the hospice? What was her prognosis? Being unable to speak her language was unsettling, especially since we were meeting for the first time on such an intimate level. As a wordsmith, words were often a comfortable way to show my heart—or enter another's.

I beckoned one of our i-to-i guides to help me translate. "Could you ask Gay how old she is?" I asked. "She is twenty-seven," he softly responded. "Has she lost any other family members to AIDS?"

"No."

"Does she have any children?"

"No, she does not."

More silence. Hmmm...not much of a connection there.

I hoped my touch spoke volumes. I wondered if someone noticed her beauty and flooded her with appreciation before she fell ill. Was she loved? Does she have any regrets? I felt torn for her, but she, interestingly, felt only still, calm.

Somehow Gay's peacefulness seeped into my hands, my heart, my thoughts. And I really began to see how lovely she was, how magnificent, really. It didn't matter what had happened before this moment or what we could or couldn't talk about. I could— I had the privilege of—showing up fully for her—and myself.

Everything Else Falls Away

As I massaged Gay's smooth soles, I no longer wondered where they'd been or where they could have taken her. I wasn't uncomfortable or unsure. The silence, it's good. Together, we were in a quiet, sacred place, and everything else fell away. When I sensed it was time to go, I looked up one more time, met Gay's eyes, and bowed. "Thank you for showing me how to love better," I said. Gay's eyes widened and shimmered when our guide translated. A golden cage door under my ribs opened.

Father Mike was right: this was a place to live. For more than the patients.

The next night, Thanksgiving night, on the houseboat after dark, I enjoyed watching Evan telling stories, his hands waving in the night air, with people from Thailand, the United States, England, and France. I hoped he'd always love this kind of experience. I hoped that some of our celebration would wrap around Gay as she slept.

For the rest of the trip, we volunteers often talked about whether such short stints of volunteering can really make a tangible difference. Can they really ease suffering, erase stigmas, and help diminish diseases that orphan millions of kids? Or do we just channel a bit of our own Mother Teresa for a while and feel virtuous when we cocoon back into our own worlds? Is it enough to try and help—or is it just a Band-Aid on an open wound that needs so much more to stem it?

"Occasionally in life there are those moments of unutterable fulfillment, which cannot be completely explained by those symbols called words. Their meanings can only be articulated by the inaudible language of the heart."

—Dr. Martin Luther King, Jr.

A Letter from Father Mike

When I got home, I Googled Father Mike and was even more in awe of what I read about him: "Compassion goes beyond religion, beyond culture, beyond nationality, beyond ethnic background. It's a way that unites us," he'd said in a *Syracuse Post-Standard* article.

At Christmas, with snow covering my piece of Colorado, he reminded me of this in an eight-page handwritten letter, his kindness lifting off each page. "You remember visiting Gay, who was a beautiful, gentle woman?" Father Mike wrote. "She died last week, as the HIV virus affected her stomach and intestinal tract, making it impossible for her to eat. What I shall always remember about her is that the day before she died, I went over to her, sat down on her bed, and I grasped her hand just to be with her, letting her know that she is not alone and that we care about her. Gay then asked me if I was coming back again tomorrow to see her, and I told her I would most certainly come and be with her. At that moment, her face seemed to lighten up with the most beautiful, wide, peaceful, gentle smile I had ever seen her give before.

"It was her way of saying good-bye and that she was peaceful and ready to accept death, whenever it would come. I participated in her cremation ceremony in the days following as we sent her on the journey to a new life."

I read on: "Gay taught me that the most important thing in life is to be truly present to one another. Just to be here for another has its own rewards and blessings. It is not how much we do but how much we are present to others that truly makes a difference."

Much of Gay's life will remain a mystery. And it doesn't matter, not in the least. I discovered all I needed to know about Gay in that afternoon in November. I discovered that beyond words and thoughts, far beyond regrets and unrealized plans and great successes, there is a place where we all meet. And are invited to be there for each other.

One Volunteer's Journey: After Coming Home

This story's another answer to the question, "Over the long haul, can volunteers really make a difference?"

Dr. Cornelia Santschi first visited the Lopburi hospice on an i-to-i humanitarian tour in 2005. "That first trip allowed me to break through my own barriers of fear and insecurity, to find the courage to step outside my comfort zones and creatively surmount new obstacles," she says.

She also stepped back, appreciated the hospice work, and saw that the staff, though dedicated, was in short supply of not only doctors but equipment. Dr. Santschi wondered what she could do to help the staff and ease the physical pain of those dying. She donated an oxygen saturation machine. But her connection to the project went to a deeper level, and she thought about how it might be challenging to engage other people back in the United States. Hospices aren't necessary glitzy, feel-good projects. They may make some really uncomfortable.

"It is not easy to stand in the face of death with grace

and humility in the midst of great suffering and pain. In our Western culture, death is generally not embraced comfortably as an inevitable part of life," Dr. Santschi says. "It is more often something we'd rather not contemplate too heavily and try to avoid until it is no longer possible. That these patients, some in their last hours of life, allowed me to share in a very real way their dying process inspired for me incredible gratitude. How better to be present with the reality of this moment than with someone who has so few moments left?"

When she returned to her practice in New York, Dr. Santschi went on to found Anatta, a nonprofit that donates medical equipment, medicines, and funds for the hospice and supports Saraburi Home For Girls, a nearby orphanage, as well as other projects. Dr. Santschi returned to Thailand several more times, once bringing a small group of friends willing to support her efforts.

This is how she makes a positive difference and becomes a fuller version of herself. We each can find our own way. "It's for each of us to break down the fears and insecurities, which hold us back from aspiring to our full potential, with tolerance and respect for the world around us," says Dr. Santschi. "If I can in some small way exemplify this, I am greatly rewarded."

OTHER OPPORTUNITIES ABROAD: DELIVER CLEAN WATER TO ONE BILLION AND MORE

If easing sickness and disease isn't your thing, you might be drawn to helping the more than one billion people who have no safe drinking water. Waterborne diseases and deaths from them are rampant in the developing world, because people don't have safe, affordable, sustainable drinking water. Many are forced to drink from open sources, rivers, or unprotected wells. Check out these groups working toward solutions.

 Water for People: Become a World Water Corps member, and support water development projects in Bolivia, Nicaragua, Guatemala, Honduras, Ecuador, Malawi, or India. Water for People helps people in developing countries improve their quality of life by supporting the development of locally sustainable drinking water resources, sanitation facilities, and health- and hygiene-education programs. If you volunteer as a World Water Corps member, the organization will match your skills with the specific needs and requirements of its country programs. www.waterforpeople.org

"What I learned from my encounters with my Buddhist sisters and brothers is that we are all one as human beings, called to live in the present moment to share the gift of compassion with everyone, no matter where we are. This understanding has deepened my own Catholic Christian faith and made me a more open person in the awareness that we have so much to learn from everyone."

—*Father Michael Bassano,*
now working with HIV-positive
people in Africa

❧ **Appropriate Infrastructure Development Group:** Take a TecoTour—an international service-learning program—and help rural villages in Guatemala access sanitation, clean water, and electricity thorough environmentally sound and affordable technologies. You can volunteer with the design, fabrication, installation, and marketing of appropriate technology products, including water filters, rain capture, composting toilets, and other technologies ranging from solar systems to windmills. www.aidg.org

❧ **Earthwatch:** This premiere organization (described in greater detail on p. 134) offers opportunities to work with scientists on field research and conservation projects, including water-mapping projects. www.earthwatch.org

"We shall not defeat AIDS, tuberculosis, malaria, or any of the other infectious diseases that plague the developing world until we have also won the battle for safe drinking water, sanitation, and basic health care."

—*Former UN Secretary-General Kofi Annan*

❧ **Amigos de las Américas:** Be aware that many volunteer-vacation organizations weave in some water projects, or at least water and sanitation education, into their trips. For instance, Amigos de las Américas works in Paraguay to build latrines in different communities and offer educational activities for families on latrine maintenance. It also offers education about water sanitation in most of its projects and builds water cisterns in many of its communities. www.amigoslink.org

Here's an account from David Beach, a volunteer who went to Honduras to map the need for clean water and sanitation interventions in a small Honduran village—and then, after improvements were made, returned to see the real difference that water and sanitation can bring to people's lives.

One Volunteer's Journey: Water Corps Changed My Life

As I was flipping through the *Florida Water Resources Journal* in early 2007, a small ad caught my eye—and changed my life. Water for People was looking for volunteers for a mapping and assessment trip to Honduras. The mission was to identify rural communities that might benefit from improved access to safe drinking water and sanitation. As a longtime Water for People supporter, I saw this as an opportunity to participate with the organization on a more personal level. I thought my background in the construction of water and wastewater projects, coupled with my training as a civil engineer, might make me a good fit for the assignment.

Arriving in Honduras

In many ways I felt that I had entered another time and dimension. While the lush countryside is beautiful, it serves as a mask for the harsh living conditions. Travel was difficult, and the people of the communities we reached were desperately poor. Water resources in many communities amounted to nothing more than a slow trickle flowing out of a mountainside, often many miles away over rugged terrain. I learned that during the dry season, those precarious sources simply dry up.

Daily life in these communities is dictated by the effort required to gather an adequate supply of water to meet family needs. We eagerly prepared our report with the hope that resources would soon make their way to these communities. I was hooked. The experience of being a World Water Corps member gave me a new perspective. Not only was it an adventure to a new and exciting part of the world, but it opened my eyes to see just how vitally important access to water can be.

My second trip to Honduras came a few months later. The assignment was to monitor past Water for People projects to assess their success (or shortcomings) and long-term sustainability. What a different trip this proved to be!

From Water Fetchers to Full-Time Students

In communities with the benefit of reliable, safe water, life was so much easier. The contrast was startling. People had time for activities that improved their lives. One day, for example, our group offered a ride to five teenagers who were on their way to school. Ordinarily they would walk for an hour and a half each day to attend high school, so they were happy with a bumpy truck ride. Each school day, they left their village at 3:30 p.m. and walked down the mountain to the next town. School was from 5:00 p.m. to 9:00 p.m. After school they walked back up the mountain, often arriving at home after 11:00 p.m. We were astonished and gratified that they were so committed to their education and realized that they might not be able to attend classes at all if they were required to help obtain their family's water.

Throughout Honduras, people were unfailingly appreciative of Water for People's efforts and eager to do what they could to help improve their own situations. Although they have so little, they were anxious to offer any comforts they could.

You Can Drink the Water

One sweltering afternoon in the last village on our trip, we were invited to sit on the front porch of the home of one of the local water-committee members. He whispered something to his daughter, who ran down the street and returned in a short time with a packet of Kool-Aid. They immediately went to work, preparing a pitcher for us. My partner and I looked at each other, each thinking of the mantra we were taught back home: "Never drink the water!" We couldn't pass up the gracious hospitality and gratefully drank it down. We enjoyed their smiles as much as we did the beverage. And no, we didn't get sick. The water—and the Kool-Aid—were excellent.

I am at the point in my career when I want a new challenge and a chance to be a part of something bigger than my small space. The enduring importance of this program is indisputable, and I feel privileged to be chosen to participate in its work. Why don't you join us? There's plenty of room for you, too.

Helping Out from Home: Support Global Health Projects and Initiatives Right Where You Are

There are literally tens of thousands of organizations lighting up the global health landscape that would be pumped to have your talents, time, and resources. If you engage with their vibrant network of volunteers and supporters around the world, you just might find a kindred community—and save some amazing lives in the

"I feel it's my duty as a world citizen."

—*Philip Burgi,*
a Colorado civil engineer who
volunteered with Water for
People's World Water Corps. His
team visited 120 Bolivian communities
in ten days to assess water
and sanitation needs.

process. Come join the collective community of millions all across the earth who are electrifying and unifying the search for solutions to everything from AIDS to polluted water.

Orphans Against AIDS: Fifteen million kids have lost one or both parents to HIV/AIDS. Join forces with Andrew Klaber, who spent a summer in Thailand and was stunned to see teenage girls forced into prostitution after their parents died of AIDS. He founded Orphans Against AIDS, which annually supports scholarships for children affected by HIV/AIDS in China, Kenya, Ghana,

> "I am at the point in my career when I want a new challenge and a chance to be a part of something bigger than my small space."
>
> —David Beach

Sierra Leone, South Africa, Uganda, and Thailand. "Today the most remarkable young people are the social entrepreneurs, those who see a problem in society and roll up their sleeves to address it in new ways," wrote Nicholas Kristof in a recent *New York Times* column that mentioned Orphans Against AIDS. www.orphansagainstaids.org

Malaria No More: Become a member of the awesome Malaria No More network. Plan an event at your school or in your community to raise awareness and funds to help save lives in Africa. The website for Malaria No More provides extensive information on how to get involved, including a fund-raising tool kit you can download to help get you started. This organization is dedicated to ending deaths due to malaria in Africa. Its goal is to engage the private sector in providing lifesaving anti-malaria bed nets and other interventions to families in Africa, while also raising the profile of the disease among policymakers, businesses, and the public. Malaria No More works in Mali, Nigeria, Uganda, Angola, Zambia, and Madagascar. *American Idol* stars Melinda Doolittle and Jordin Sparks have recently teamed up with Malaria No More to help distribute nets in Africa and raise money for those in need. A donation of $10 can provide one long-lasting, insecticide-treated anti-malaria bed net to an African country in need. There are other ways to help as well. www.malarianomore.org

❧ **Stayin' Alive:** A simple but powerful stroke of genius, Stayin' Alive was conceived by a group of high-school students in Florida. It uses school dances around the country to raise awareness and funds to fight malaria. The program is spreading nationwide quickly, and Malaria No More is partnering with ten thousand Stayin' Alive dances nationwide to raise $10 million. The money will secure one million anti-malaria bed nets, protecting two million children, the organization says. www.malarianomore.org/stayinalive

❧ **Nothing But Nets:** Donate nets, and find or start a Netraiser Team in your area. Nothing But Nets fights malaria in Africa through the distribution of bed nets to those in need. The creation of the campaign began with a column in *Sports Illustrated* by Rick Reilly, encouraging each of his readers to donate $10 to purchase an anti-malaria bed net.

The response was so overwhelming that it led to a nationwide movement to raise awareness and funds for the suffering people of Africa.

The Nothing But Nets website provides all the info you need to get started. www.nothingbutnets.net

❧ **World AIDS Day:** Participate in this annual event December 1. If there's not an event in your community, consider organizing one. Or how about writing a guest opinion to raise awareness? www.worldaidsday.org

❧ **World Water Day:** Raise awareness of the clean water and sanitation issue. Organize an event for World Water Day (March 20) or support an existing one. www.worldwaterday.net.

&o **Water 1st:** Water 1st supports the implementation of community-implemented and community-managed sustainable water-supply and sanitation projects in the developing world. www.water1st.org

&o **Tap Project:** Another really cool project: dine at a Tap Project participating restaurant during World Water Week. Tap Project restaurants will invite their customers to donate a minimum of $1 for the tap water they would normally get for free. For every dollar raised, a child will have clean drinking water for forty days. The Tap Project is a campaign that celebrates clean and accessible tap water and helps UNICEF provide safe drinking water to children around the world. www.tapproject.org

&o **Elton John AIDS Foundation:** This foundation has quietly supported HIV/AIDS grassroots initiatives in fifty-five countries. It supports HIV/AIDS prevention and education programs, as well as programs that provide direct care and other services for people living with HIV/AIDS. www.ejaf.org

&o **Stephen Lewis Foundation:** This organization focuses on women, orphans, grandmothers, and people living with HIV/AIDS. It funds more than 140 projects in fifteen sub-Saharan African countries. One of its standouts: Grandmothers to Grandmothers, a galvanized network of grandmothers across Canada who have raised more than $1 million for grandmothers in Africa who bury their own children and then raise their orphaned grandchildren. The support helps the African grandmothers afford school fees, food, community gardens, small animals, and dignified burials for their loved ones, among other necessities. www.stephenlewisfoundation.org

ஃ **Water Advocates:** Engage with this nonprofit organization working to increase support for worldwide access to safe, affordable, and sustainable supplies of drinking water and adequate sanitation. Whether you're representing yourself, a school, church, corporation, or some other entity, its site offers effective ways you can help raise awareness and boost funding for effective water, sanitation, and hygiene projects. Water Advocates also offers a full list of U.S.-based nonprofits working for safe, affordable, sustainable drinking water and basic sanitation facilities that can use your support, from Catholic Relief Services and Rotary International to Global Water Challenge and Save the Children. www.wateradvocates.org

ஃ **Partners in Health:** Donate, raise awareness, or volunteer to support Partners in Health, launched by Dr. Paul Farmer, which addresses malaria, AIDS, and tuberculosis. PIH sometimes needs volunteers for tasks ranging from data entry to translation at its Boston office. You can also donate medical equipment if it's in excellent condition, fully operational, and electrically compatible. www.pih.org

ஃ **Project C.U.R.E:** Donate medical equipment and supplies to this humanitarian powerhouse. The Commission of Urgent Relief and Equipment, Project C.U.R.E., is the world's largest volume distributor of donated medical equipment. It's sent more than 825 cargo containers to at least 105 countries around the world. Ethiopia just got its first heart-catheter lab, thanks to Project C.U.R.E. Read more about this organization's mission on its website, and see if your community has equipment and supplies to support its efforts. You can also volunteer at a web of collection centers, helping sort and manage donations, in Phoenix, Nashville, Houston, or at Project C.U.R.E.'s Denver headquarters. www.projectcure.org

  ❧ **The William J. Clinton Foundation:** President Clinton created the William J. Clinton Foundation to strengthen the capacity of people around the world to meet the challenges of global interdependence. A centerpiece of its works has been the Clinton Foundation HIV/AIDS Initiative, which brings treatment to hundreds of thousands of underserved populations. The foundation sometimes seeks volunteers with business, communication, proposal writing, HIV/AIDS clinical care, and other assignments/internships here and in the developing world. www.clintonfoundation.org

  ❧ **Millennium Promise:** Started by Columbia University professor Jeffrey Sachs, this organization operates with the premise that extreme poverty can be eliminated in our lifetime. It encourages others to engage around global poverty, disease, and hunger and has created the UN Millennium Project to sponsor eighty Millennium Villages in ten sub-Saharan African countries. Each village consists of about five thousand people and will demonstrate what it takes to meet the UN Millennium Development Goals on a large scale. Millennium Promise is also partnering with Building with Books to build thirty-two additional schools in Mali and Senegal. You can support the organization in many ways, including joining the Join the You + Village Campaign. Your support will help sponsor the villages and buy malaria bed nets, as well as seeds and fertilizers for enterprising farmers who want to support themselves. It will also help create new, clean water wells and other projects. www.millenniumpromise.org

🐚 **ONE:** Join the ONE Campaign and make poverty history. Visit the ONE Campaign website and check out their volunteer tool kit, which invites you to do everything from organizing letter and call-in campaigns for Congress to organizing an event to raise awareness. World AIDS Day is December 1—that's a great time to be in solidarity with millions worldwide focused on this issue. www.one.org

🐚 **Keep a Child Alive:** Alicia Key's organization provides medical services and clinics to make HIV/AIDS treatment possible. Less than 5 percent of children have access to lifesaving ARVs, and Keep a Child Alive is addressing this shortfall. You can support the organization and help build a medical clinic or orphanage, or provide funding for nurses, doctors, medical equipment, clean linens, and other supplies to bring the clinics up to scale. www.kcabeta.org

🐚 **Global Citizen Corps:** Join this national movement of passionate young people who think and act globally on poverty. Global Citizen Corps leaders organize Global Action Days in their schools and communities around the issues of HIV/AIDS, hunger, climate change, and access to education. They raise awareness among their classmates, raise their voices in the media, raise money, and lobby elected officials. www.globalcitizencorps.org

What Do You Think? Taking a Bite Out of Malaria

There's a raging debate in the global health community. Malaria kills at least three thousand children a day. Many families in Africa, Asia, and other malaria-thick regions don't have an anti-malaria bed net to protect themselves from malaria-carrying mosquitoes. Handing over $1 to buy a bed net is just not possible when it could be spent on food or lifesaving medicine.

What is the best way to get bed nets to the people who need them? Is it best to dispatch nonprofits, church groups, mission workers, and others to donate and distribute bed nets as quickly as possible? Or should the market forces be allowed to work—with private enterprises springing up to manufacture and sell bed nets? What would you advocate if the decision came down to you?

Here's how a recent BusinessWeek article framed the debate: "On one side are believers in the traditional aid model, who say that bed nets should be given away for free by governments and nonprofits to reach the maximum number of people as quickly as possible. On the other side are backers of so-called social marketing, who argue that bringing businesses into the mix improves efficiency and adds incentives and economic benefits to doing good. Harnessing the private sector, they say, creates self-reliance—not dependence."

Other people advocate combining donation-driven efforts with market-driven ones. What do you think is best?

Helping in the United States: Improving Health Care and Easing Poverty Here

🐾 **The AIDS Health Project:** This San Francisco–based non-profit has championed HIV support and services since 1984. It needs volunteers to help with everything from support-group leadership to HIV testing. www.ucsf-ahp.org

🐾 **Habitat for Humanity:** Help build quality, affordable homes for low-income families. You can join the Gulf Recovery Effort, which helps victims of Hurricane Katrina; Women Build, which trains women to build homes together in a comfortable and supportive environment; youth programs for ages five to twenty-five; disaster response teams; and more. Anyone is welcome, whether you have experience in construction or not. www. habitat.org.

There are at least 3.5 million homeless people in the United States—plus some five million kids who still go to bed hungry each night. Here are some projects you can support to volunteer and help feed the hungry and homeless.

> *A few years ago, we traveled to a hospital in Mozambique, where we met a young girl who was sick with malaria, shivering with fever, and on the verge of death. I remember looking down in her crib and thinking that if this were an American child, she wouldn't be suffering."*
>
> —*Melinda Gates*

🐄 **Heifer International:** Heifer International, which works to end hunger and poverty around the world, has helped more than forty-five million people since 1944. It's also active throughout the United States. It provides livestock and environmentally sound agricultural training to improve the lives of people who struggle for reliable sources of food and income. For instance, it works in Appalachia to help young people learn small-scale farming techniques.

Heifer hopes to help twenty-three million more families move toward greater self-reliance in the next decade. You can volunteer as a Heifer Community Volunteer to spread the word about Heifer throughout your schools, congregations, and communities. Want to volunteer or help raise funds for Heifer in your own community? Visit the Heifer International website to find the regional office closest to you. www.heifer.org

🐄 **Common Ground:** Want to help homeless and low-income people get back on their feet? Look into supporting this organization, which provides permanent, affordable housing and on-site social services. Common Ground's housed more than four thousand homeless and low-income people in New

York and Connecticut and now is branching into fifteen other cities. Common Ground is proud that its housing units cost a fraction of what's spent on emergency shelter, incarceration, or emergency medical care. www.commonground.org

&o **Amizade:** Sign on to volunteer at the Washington, D.C., Central Kitchen, which serves the homeless and offers culinary job training for unemployed men and women. www.amizade.org

&o **Share Our Strength:** For twenty years, nationally renowned chefs have supported Share Our Strength's Taste of the Nation events across the country, which have collectively raised more than $70 million to end childhood hunger. Contact your local Taste of the Nation organizers, and offer your services. Whether you're a chef, fund-raiser, or willing to set up and bus tables, they will put you to work. www.taste.strength.org

One Volunteer's Journey: Diving in—Literally—So the Uninsured Get Health Care

If you want to make a difference right where you live, how about offering your time, talent, and treasure to those struggling to live without health insurance? Check in with your area's free medical clinic, and see what they might need in terms of volunteering, fund-raising, or supplies, from medical equipment to toys and books for the waiting room. Maybe they could use your voice for building awareness. Maybe they could use your ability to inspire and rally other people, which John Heineman did when he learned that forty-seven million Americans—including about eight million children—had no health insurance. Introduced in the first chapter, Heineman was shocked to find out how many hard-working families had no access to health insurance, so he rallied support for the Iowa City Free Medical Clinic by training for and swimming the English Channel in the summer of 2007. "The most difficult part of the swim was my view of endless water," he recalls. "The waves were so big that I could not see much of any-thing but water—making me feel as if I were going nowhere. However, shoals of jellyfish helped amuse me as I tried to dodge the purple jellies and the brown jellies, which were the stingers. But I was still hit in the face and extremities many times. My younger broth-er and swim coach, Thomas, kept me entertained by scribbling messages on a white board in the fishing trawler I was following to keep me motivated in the seemingly endless water."

After eight to nine hours of swimming, Heineman said his body began to break down its fat reserves and the salty water made his throat swell, making it almost im-possible to drink fluids and eat bits of bananas or Mars bars. Plus, the chop of the water got even more violent as he neared France.

The most fun part of the swim, he says, was about the last fifty meters from the French shore: "The water finally calmed, and the waves subsided. As I washed up on the sandy Cap New Bris beach, I heard some celebrations out in the boat but was too exhausted to do much myself. It felt so good to touch and feel solid ground. It made me realize how much I appreciate living a terrestrial life! I rubbed some sand in my Crossing for Care wristband, said a short prayer, and swam back to the dingy, because I couldn't stay on French soil without a passport for more than five minutes!"

In the end, it wasn't easy for Heineman to dip his toe into the fund-raising waters, either. But the more he spoke out about the needs of the uninsured, reminding people that no one deserves to go without health coverage and that no one's immune from falling into the "un-insurance cracks" until there's a health-care revolution, the more support streamed in from around the country. Eventually, he raised $19,000 for the clinic and along the way has met priceless people served by the clinic. Those people, he says, are "his exposure to humanity at its finest."

Like a mother and her daughters who approached him at a fund-raiser: "She expressed her gratitude for the clinic during a rough patch in her life when she was without insurance, going through a divorce, unemployed, caring for one child, and expecting another. She said she was not sure she would have gone through with her youngest daughter's birth had it not been for the free care she received. But she'd gone on to get her teaching degree and was now teaching at an elementary school. Her daughters were now healthy and vibrant. In fact, the youngest wanted me to come and watch her swim at the city pool, because she'd passed her Red Cross swimming lessons with flying colors!"

CHAPTER SIX

Touch the World

Preserve Endangered Animals and Habitats/Reforest the World

"People talk too much. We're no longer talking; we are working. The challenge now is to tell the world to go dig holes and plant seedlings."

—*Professor Mangari Maathai,*
founder of Kenya's Green Belt Movement, which has planted
more than thirty million trees in twelve African countries.

"I'm in love, I'm in love, I'm in love with a wonderful wallaby!" Jane Stanfield gushed on her blog after waking at 6:00 a.m. to bottle feed the animals, rake their prodigious poo pellets by day, and sleep in a metal shed with mosquito netting by night. It's another day of poo patrol, and Stanfield makes a game of it: "I tell myself I'm on an extensive Easter egg hunt. Other days, I tell the wallabies I am their cleaning woman coming in after their party."

Over a two-week stay in the Australian outback through an i-to-i volunteer stint, Stanfield mucked, fed, and nurtured wallabies, koalas, flying squirrels, and wombats. Getting peed on or being ankle-deep in waste was all part of the adventure. In fact, she adores animals so much, she went on to volunteer with lions, penguins, and baboons in South Africa—which she describes as "physically exhausting yet so rewarding. They are so humanlike. And after four weeks, I had really developed relationships with them."

Do you swoon over animals and love the outdoors? Is there more than a bit of Stanfield in you? Do you worship the ground Jane Goodall walks on? Watch Animal Planet and the Nature Channel religiously?

Stanfield actually spent an entire year traveling and giving back, calling it her "year of living generously." The creatures of the jungles, oceans, and other natural ecosystems are like a magnet for many volunteers. If you're one of them, pay attention to that call of the wild: it easily could be your entry point to giving back. Many people find they aren't all that interested in serving people all day long, but the thought of spending days helping penguins, macaws, or rare, red-faced monkeys makes them howl with joy.

Ecotourism, or environmentally focused volunteer vacations or trips, can combine conservation, environmental protection, and research. These kinds of volunteer stints are on the rise and range from communing with iguanas in the Galapagos to planting trees on the slopes of Mount Kilimanjaro to curb massive deforestation.

Typically, you can assume that some of these offerings will be more rugged and physically strenuous than standard volunteer trips—and take you off the beaten path, for sure. You may have to (get to!) sleep in tents or tree platforms or hammocks in the wild, wake in the middle of the night to record nocturnal animal behavior, or carry buckets from rivers to water new saplings.

Is your heart still beating high? Wishing you could be in that Amazon hammock or boat on the Indian Ocean right now? Dashing to the closet to excavate your hiking boots? There's no better way to fall in love with the amazing creatures with which we share this planet, no more hands-on way to help reforest a world swiftly losing its forests.

Here's Your Challenge: The World Has Lost More than 80 Percent of Its Original Forests in the Last Century

To make up for the loss of trees, some estimate that an area as large as Peru—or about fourteen billion trees a year—would have to be planted. Meanwhile, deforestation threatens the extinction of one hundred animal species a day. Thousands of species of animals, from rare butterflies to baboons, are now endangered. Also at risk? Asian elephants, Amur leopards, Sumatran tigers, Chilean flamingos, and many other species.

ONE TARGET TO SHOOT FOR

The UN Millennium Development Goals challenge us to "reverse the loss of environmental resources and reduce biodiversity loss, achieving, by 2010, a significant reduction in the rate of loss." But why stop then? Let's keep working to create a world that works for everyone, including the ecosystems and all the creatures they sustain, pandas to peacocks. If you want to roll up your sleeves and pant legs, throw on your waders, and dive into these beautiful animals' worlds, here are a few representative opportunities.

Here's Your Opportunity

WADE INTO THE WILDERNESS, SAVE ANIMALS, AND RESTORE HABITATS

❧ **Greenforce:** Volunteer at the world's largest panda reserve in China, doing everything from preparing carrots, apples, and bamboo to feeding pandas and helping scientists collect behavior data. Or consider living with and working alongside the Massai in Africa, where Massai warriors will teach you how to track animals from giraffes to zebras. They'll also teach you about their culture and teach you some basic Maasai words. You'll help collect data on the animals to help the local people and animals live in balance. www.greenforceusa.org

❧ **Earthwatch:** Directly assist scientists in research or conservation projects in the field, from tracking the habits of rare animals in Madagascar to ensure their survival to helping monitor and protect Amazon dolphins, giant river otters, monkeys, exotic birds and butterflies, lions, and countless other wild creatures. This is one organization that allows you to fully immerse in the wildest, most wonderful places on Earth.

You can help unravel the survival strategies of an ancient egg-laying mammal and large monitor lizard in Kangaroo Island or observe meerkat behavior in South Africa. You can identify and monitor nearly two hundred species of butterflies in Vietnam or survey and care for cheetahs in Namibia. Here's a great description of the Santa Lucia Reserve project: "Home to tremendous biodiversity including mammals such as Andean cats, pumas, coatimundis, spectacled bears, ocelots, and even the occasional jaguar. In this protected cloud forest, you'll hike through mountainous terrain with a different research assignment each day. Teams will help establish and maintain camera traps, i.e., cameras set up to snap photos when triggered by animal movements. You'll also help identify and photograph animal tracks around the traps. Each team will help with collecting aerial images by using a remote-controlled helicopter, and then groundtruthing the images by matching them to the crowns of trees in the forest. At sites that are aerially photographed, you'll also gather data on the habitat by measuring and counting trees, determining canopy cover, and identifying the species of orchids and other plant life. In your recreational time, you can play pickup games of soccer or volleyball, enjoy fiestas and dances in nearby towns, swim in the river, or hike to waterfalls."

Or if Africa calls to you, consider a new "Walking with African Animals" expedition in South Africa. You'll walk through classic acacia woodland, bushveld, and forest, beginning at the crack of dawn, to observe wildlife. This is a rare chance to walk through scenery most people only see from a Land Rover. The South African bush can be your backyard for a while, the organization says. And "nothing compares to the sound of a distant lion as you drift off to sleep." www.earthwatch.org

i-to-i: If you love animals and getting your hands dirty, i-to-i has a host of offerings: Support monkeys in South Africa, close to the wilderness of the famed Kruger National Park. You'll help care for injured or orphaned monkeys and do some general maintenance at the Vervet Monkey Foundation center, which looks after more than five hundred monkeys. Or in Costa Rica you can support marine turtle conservation projects, including the endangered leatherback turtles. More than 80 percent of the leatherback turtle population has been lost in the past ten years. You'll get trained on marine turtles and help with research and data collection. www.i-to-i.com

&o **GeoVisions:** Here's a great chance to support the big game animals in South Africa with a Safari Tented Camp as your base. Working alongside trained staff, you may get to monitor wildlife and fences, conduct game counts, help conserve and maintain a national park—including repairing areas suffering from soil erosion—and participate in classes on South African society and culture, coastal conservation, and ecology. Enjoy relaxing at the beaches and whale watching in your leisure. www.geovisions.org

&o **Projects Abroad:** Go to the Peruvian rainforest to live in the heart of the Amazon jungle, and participate in a variety of work aimed at sustaining and protecting this incredible environment. You'll work on sustainable agricultural projects in collaboration with the local indigenous community, as well as wild-animal re-release programs and construction and trail maintenance, and you'll monitor biodiversity from a forty-two-meter canopy walkway to record the positive effect this project has had on the jungle ecosystem. In South Africa, work at a conservation program based in a nature reserve that spans the Limpopo River border with Botswana, where volunteers live among wild game while conserving local ecosystems and collecting scientific data used to set policy regarding poaching, bush clearing, and border control. Depending on the time of year, you could be tracking leopard, lion, African wild dog (Cape Hunting dog), or elephant, and helping to rehabilitate baobab trees, fever trees, or "Njala" trees. Or support the endangered sea turtles on the Pacific coast of Mexico. Working mainly at night when the turtles lay their eggs, you can collect sea turtle eggs, take them to a safe area, and rebury them until they mature. Some nights you will watch the nests that were buried six weeks earlier and have the amazing experience of watching the hatchlings as they crawl out of the nest and protecting them as they head for the ocean. www. projects-abroad.org

Global Volunteer Projects: Always been interested in working with pandas? Go to China and work at a reserve that protects giant pandas. After a period of training, you'll help with general maintenance of the pandas' living area, including preparing their daily meals. Pandas eat more than bamboo, so you'll help prepare and serve them fruit, vegetables, and even specially formulated "panda bread." The project may also need volunteers in other areas, including helping produce information for visitors. Or head to Ghana and help maintain Kakum National Park rehabilitating and developing the jungle trails where forty species of large animals live, including a population of rare African forest elephants. You can also go to Mexico and help protect sea turtles, collecting their eggs from nesting sites, putting them in incubators safe from predators, and when they're ready for hatching, taking them back to their nests and enjoying and monitoring them as they make it back to the ocean. www.globalvolunteerprojects.org

✆ **Global Volunteer Network:** In Honduras, work off the coast on the beautiful Caribbean island of Utila at an iguana center, dedicated to the protection and breeding of the Utila iguana. Or work at a reserve, conserving endangered manatees on the Caribbean near the port town of La Ceiba. www. globalvolunteernetwork.com

Kris Dreesen was a Volunteer on Team I, 2006, an Earthwatch project in the Amazon.

One Volunteer's Journey: An Amazon Riverboat Exploration

We walk along the machete-blazed path, our footsteps padding along the fallen leaves and dirt. Leaf-cutter ants haul pieces of dime-sized greenery across the trail in a straight line, military style. We hike quietly and slowly so we don't spook the animals and don't miss anything during the two or three miles in.

We will rest for an hour then hike back, counting monkeys, wild pigs, and other large mammals that may cross our path. What we see will be combined with sightings by biologists and volunteers over several months to estimate how many species are in Lago Preto, including the endangered red uakari monkeys. I wonder if we'll see a uakari. The highest concentration of red uakaris in the world is right outside our houseboat, but I'm one of the only volunteers who hasn't seen one.

It's my last day of field research, my last chance. Juan, our local guide, led us on the trail. Soon, Juan stops. He looks at us and points to a cluster of trees about forty yards away. I see some movement, some fur. Uakari? Squirrel monkeys. Lots of them.

They are crossing the trail in the treetops, tails pitched high in the air like prancing cats. One by one, they emerge through the branches. A few stop a second to look down and check out their visitors. Juan says it was a troop of twenty, with four capuchins tagging along. He and the other guides are amazing. Juan sees things we don't and hears things we never will. He grew up on the river; the Amazon is his backyard. Sometimes he lives out here on a platform for months.

He watches over the Lago Preto concession area, bringing only sugar and rice, and spears fish for the rest of his food. In the forest now, he mimics a bird call and the bird answers. Laura and I sidestep ruts of mud, then give up and enjoy trudging on the trail in the ankle-deep gunk. It sounds like a vacuum as it nearly sucks my hiking boots clean off. Further down the trail we are treated to another march of the same squirrel monkeys.

The plants and trees are amazing and unlike anything I've seen. Trees look like braided ropes, vines like turtle tracks and bright green spaghetti noodles. An hour in, we hear the faint "chi chi" of uakaris. Jackpot! Juan freezes and folds his hands across his mouth, imitating their call: "chi chi." They come no closer. We wait, not moving a muscle.

"Chi chi." Moments later the chatter fades into the forest. Out of luck. Juan asks me in Spanish, "Have you seen a uakari?" I shake my head. With a small wave, he flips his machete to follow him. This is never going to work, I think. The monkeys are long gone. We bushwhack through branches anyway, ducking under spider webs and studded palm trees toward where we heard the last monkey conversation.

After a few minutes, Juan stops. Ah well, we were close. He stares at the forest floor as if in defeat, then points his hand to the trees above us as if ending a concerto. I follow his fingertips up to the treetops. The uakaris! They are almost directly above us in bacacho trees, crossing to and fro, chowing down on fruit. Their fur is cinnamon, their faces cherry red. One is buttdown on a branch staring at us. He seems only vaguely distracted from his fruit by us and soon turns and takes off, swinging from branch to branch, lunging with grace and a loud rustle of leaves.

There are so few in the world, and there must be ten right here, eating lunch in the Amazon. They are too far to get a close-up look, so while I am with them, they are still a mystery. My mind flashes to the close-up photos we saw on the boat during a slide presentation. Their similarity to our own faces was startling. Now I can't make out their features, so my imagination fills them in: big brown eyes, distinct lines on the face, and a big forehead. The one above us is about the size of a Dalmatian. It soon reaches out with its arms and disappears into the trees, too. They make their way through the canopy and get further away. Some of them stop like the squirrel monkeys to check us out. This is amazing.

For a few moments, we've stepped into their world—or below it rather. I mouth, "Wow!" to Juan, who flashes me a big grin. When they move on, Juan and I mark the milestone with a photo: me with my arms up in triumph and him hanging one of his around my shoulder, machete in hand, chuckling.

REFOREST THE WORLD

If we're going to support the endangered species of the world, we have to shore up and support their habitats. Deforestation causes the extinction of a hundred species a day, according to some estimates. If building forests appeals to you, here are some opportunities.

Earthwatch: Mangrove forests are among the most productive wetland ecosystems on Earth, but they are also one of the most threatened habitats, according to Earthwatch scientists. Historically, mangrove forests lined three-quarters of all tropical and subtropical coasts. Now less than half of these forests remain, and more are lost each year to firewood production, building materials, coastal development, and shrimp fisheries. Go to Kenya with Earthwatch to live and work with local villagers, and conduct experiments to help rehabilitate degraded mangroves in Gazi Bay. Surrounded by beautiful beaches and impressive birds, among other animals, you'll plant mangrove seedlings on the beach and monitor rates of beach erosion and crab and fish populations. Or head to the Puerto Rican rain forest to measure trees, count lizards or frogs, tag and identify vine species, and help set up new experimental plots by planting different tree and shrub species. All the while, you'll hike through beautiful tropical rainforest areas, sometimes climbing up steep hillsides, sometimes following fast-flowing rivers. A night expedition will take you into the forest to help count coqui frogs. www.earthwatch.org

Earthwatch on the Move

If you question whether volunteers really can green up the face of the earth, here's just a few of Earthwatch's impressive accomplishments. Among many other things, Earthwatch volunteers have identified fifty-two new plant species in the rainforests of Cameroon, helped protect orca whales in Washington State, contributed to the development of a marine-protected area off the coast of Spain, and documented permafrost melt in the Canadian Arctic. Earthwatch says the following national parks and wildlife preserves were also created as a direct result of its volunteers' dedicated service: Tram Chim National Park, Vietnam; Sandy Point National Wildlife Reserve, St. Croix; Ischigualasto Valley World

Heritage Site, Argentina; Spanish River Provincial Park, Ontario; Playa Grande National Park, Costa Rica. For more information, check out www.earthwatch.org.

🐾 i-to-i: In Costa Rica, the remaining tropical forest, like much of the world, is being impacted each year. Join a conservation project here, and as a volunteer in the national parks, wildlife reserves, and community-based ecotourism projects, you can patrol with park rangers, help with reforestation, construct and maintain trails, support general maintenance and organic farming, or work with the local community on education programs.

You will be in one or more of the many national parks in Costa Rica, including Barra Honda, Ballena National Marine Park, Tortuguero, Carara Biological Reserve, Cabo Blanco Absolute, and Gandoca Manzanillo.

Or consider living for a while on the slopes of Mount Kenya and helping to preserve some of the rapidly diminishing indigenous and exotic trees. As you plant trees, build seedbeds, and help with facilities maintenance, you'll also get a chance to spot elephants, buffalos, waterbucks, leopards, and monkeys deep in the forest. You'll also help educate the local community about the impacts of deforestation.

Or go to Ecuador and work with the Rain Forest Concern on one of its flagship projects, Santa Lucia Cloud Forest Reserve. This project is in the amazing mountain cloud forest of the Choco Andea region of northwest Ecuador, rich with more than 1,500 species of tropical plants and 380 species of birds and exotic animals, including the endangered spectacled bear. www.i-to-i.com

&co **Globe Aware:** Journey to Jamaica's last remaining wilderness, Cockpit Country. This is a global treasure, due to its many endemic species as well as its unique karst geography. You'll help clean up local rivers, caves, and sinkholes—marking trails, implementing anti-erosion measures on hillsides, and helping with other projects. www.globeaware.org

&co **Volunteers for Peace:** This organization has thirty projects that involve reforestation, including some in Tanzania, Kenya, Ghana, and India. Ask about the other opportunities on each project, too. For instance, an Indian project goes to several villages where you'll not only work on reforestation and tree planting, but may also help spread health and hygiene awareness among the tribal villages, teach English, build playgrounds, and assist underprivileged schools. www.vfp.org

&co **Village Volunteers:** Help villagers in Kenya, Ghana, India, or Nepal find alternative fuel and ease deforestation; participate in workshops and activities for community members on subjects such as making briquettes (fuel made out of biomass that burns for eight hours); or teach biointensive organic farming techniques. www.villagevolunteers.org

QUESTIONS TO ASK

Expect many of the greener trips to be more rugged and strenuous than other voluntourism offerings, so ask lots of questions. Here's a snapshot of the kinds of things you want to know, from the Projects Abroad Conservation in South Africa project: "Accommodations are at a base camp in large but basic bedrooms surrounding a large communal area with a fire pit and kitchen facilities, where much of the food is cooked over a traditional open *braai*, a kind of barbecue. Hot-water showers and toilets are open to the sky."

The following are some other questions to ask:

- How physically demanding is the work?
- How far will I need to hike, and what will the terrain be like?
- Will I be digging ditches, putting up retaining walls, picking up trash? And if so, for how many hours a day?
- Will we need to clear roads and paths before other work can begin?
- What will my accommodations be like?
- Will I ever be sleeping in hammocks, tents, or sleeping bags on the beach?
- What's our power source?
- Who will provide our meals, and what are the hygiene standards?
- Will I have to help with the cooking and cleanup?
- Will we have hot and cold running water—or not?
- Will I get a chance to play in waterfalls, admire amazing sunsets from mountain crags, or spelunk in caves?*

---

* You'll be living for a time in some of the most exquisite settings on Earth—so be sure to ask if you'll have enough time and transportation to enjoy them. Touring a bit may not be important to you, but if it is, make sure your placement offers it. On the Earthwatch Kenya trip, for instance, you'll have time off to snorkel on a coral reef, tour historical sites, watch the dolphins—or just lie back and watch the great birds, including pelicans, palm vultures, bee-eaters, and hornbills.

Final questions:

- What's the sustainability of my project?
- Who will water and maintain the trees, for instance, when we go home?
- Are local villagers committed to this project?
- Will they be working alongside us and have some "ownership" in the project in the future?

Helping Out from Home: What Can You Do If You Can't Go to the Rainforest?

If you can't dig trees somewhere in the world, you can dig in today and support those who are. Here are some great opportunities to love the earth with more trees:

🌿 **Armenia Tree Project:** Support this project generating lots of excitement and buzz and watched by others around the world. It's planted more than two million trees, engaging great support in its planting and ongoing care from local villagers. In a show of solidarity, more than 250 families in Armenia have created tree nurseries in their own backyards to support ATP. If you send them $20, you can plant a tree in Armenia, too. If you send $5,000, you can plant a whole forest. www.armeniatree.org

🌿 **Trees for the Future:** This organization's helped thousands of villages in Asia, Africa, and Latin America plant up to fifty million trees. The organization makes it easy for you to plant trees around the world. For instance, a $100 donation plants a grove of one thousand. You can adopt a village for $480 and plant about five thousand trees. www.treesftf.org

&o **TreeGreetings:** The next time you want to send an e-card to mark a birthday, holiday, Mother's Day, or any celebration, send a TreeGreeting, the perfect blend of technology and nature. Created by longtime tree lover Ilan Shamir, TreeGreetings sends an amazing, beautiful nature e-card with music—and plants a shade, fruit, flowering, or evergreen tree in the United States or El Salvador. You can also plant a peace or blessing tree. TreeGreetings uses no paper in the process, from the sending of the card to the planting of the tree—a truly "carbon positive" gift-giving experience. Both the sender and recipient can view the planting areas and tree varieties online. The organization has planted more than three thousand trees since its inception in 2005. www.treegreetings.com

Helping in the United States: Fur Seals, Monkeys, and Bears—Oh, My

&o **Earthwatch:** Earthwatch also has many volunteer projects in the United States. You can head to Alaska and study fur seals and support the conservation of the Bering Sea, study marine mammals in California, do archeology work at a mammoth site in South Dakota, and much more. www.earthwatch.org

&o **Global Vision International:** GVI is a UK-based organization that sends volunteers on thousands of trips worldwide. It also operates an animal sanctuary project in Florida, where you can help care for rescued wildlife including big cats, bears, wolves, and monkeys. www.gvi.co.uk

🐾 **Sierra Club:** The Sierra Club hosts about ninety annual volunteer service projects across the country. Here's just a sampling: You can help support calving whales in Hawaii, maintain protected cliff dwellings once inhabited by the Pueblo Indians in Colorado, collect native seeds and scientific data in Arizona's Grand Canyon, or build trails at Cape Cod National Seashore in Massachusetts. You can also eradicate invasive plants, repair trails, or clean campgrounds at other natural sites around the country. www.sierraclub.org

🐾 **Wilderness Volunteers:** Working with the National Park Service, Forest Service, Bureau of Land Management, and the U.S. Fish and Wildlife Service, Wilderness Volunteers organizes volunteer service in the wilds here in the United States. You can choose from volunteer stints in Florida, Idaho, Oregon, California, Utah, New Mexico, Virginia, Maine, and other states. www.wildernessvolunteers.org

Join Jane Goodall's Environmental Corps: A Look at Roots and Shoots

Youth-led, youth-driven, Roots and Shoots is the Jane Goodall Foundation's hot, hip humanitarian program — one of the most exciting ways for young people of all ages to engage on environmental issues. With tens of thousands of youth in almost a hundred countries, Roots and Shoots says it connects kids "who share a desire to help make our world a better place."

Founded by sixteen African students and Jane Goodall in 1991, the organization is made up of Roots and Shoots groups in every conceivable expression, from nature centers to school groups to scout clubs. Some teachers create Roots and Shoots groups as service-learning projects based from their classrooms.

Two big Roots and Shoot campaigns that might grab your interest: (1) the Reusable Bag Campaign, designed to reduce and eventually eliminate the use of plastic bags, which cause the deaths of hundreds of thousands of sea turtles, whales, and other marine mammals each year who mistake them for food. You can buy reusable bags directly from the organization; and (2) the ReBirth the Earth/Trees for Tomorrow Campaign, which aims to raise $10,000 to build five Roots and Shoots nurseries in Tanzania, while planting three thousand trees in the United States.

Or think outside the box and create your own campaign. A Roots and Shoots group in Nepal helps children too often enslaved as domestic servants to get an education—as well as respect and a chance at freedom. Are you an expert in butterflies, elk habitats, recycling, energy conservation, or other cultures? Whatever your passion or knowledge, Roots and Shoots groups would love you to come and share what you know. And if you really love what they're doing, sign on to be a group leader, or volunteer at Roots and Shoots' regional or national offices or at its many events. Ready to travel? The organization also offers some volunteer opportunities through their offices in Tanzania and Uganda. Whatever your project becomes, be sure to share photos and success stories with other projects and youth around the world via the organization's online community.

For more info: www.rootsandshoots.org

REBUILDING WILDERNESS TRAILS AT HOME: HOW ONE VOLUNTEER ROLLS UP HIS SLEEVES

The stunning beauty of the wild, where bald eagles drift on mountain currents and brown bears herd their cubs, often leads Vernon Cook to exchange his Kentucky medical school post for a shovel, backpack, and sleeping bag. An associate medical professor at the University of Louisville, Cook has volunteered with or led more than twenty-five trips to places like Idaho's Hells Canyon and Seven Devils Wilderness Area and Oregon's Eagle Cap Wilderness.

With bighorn sheep and mountain goats sometimes perched on crags above them, Cook and his volunteers with Wilderness Volunteers, Sierra Club, or American Hiking Society clear trails of boulders, downed trees, and logs, sometimes skirting prodigious bear scat as they work. Often the trails are in sorry shape due to increasing federal cutbacks.

Cook says he often asks himself why he so often leaves his comfortable home to sleep in the outback a thousand miles away with strangers. Why not just do good locally in Louisville? Why not do any thousands of other things? "This work brings out the tried and true part of me that comes from peasant stock, from the generations of immigrants in my family," he says. "I like to dive in with my hands outdoors, and these trips are an outlet for that part of me.

"I also like John F. Kennedy's quote, 'Ask not what your country can do for you, but what you can do for your country.'"

Another pull he can't resist: the amazing people he's had a chance to volunteer alongside. "The people who volunteer to work on these trips are the best sort of down-to-earth, wholesome folks," says Cook. "They come from all walks of life and usually have their lives together. On a Mammoth Cave National Park trip in Kentucky, we had three sisters, ages sixty-eight to seventy-five, who volunteered. They all had a great time and worked hard."

Volunteers also have to know themselves and trust they can assimilate to the outdoors with other volunteers, he says: "You know you're getting close and have bonded when, toward the end of the week, you're all searching for ticks on each other."

But clearing trails in the outback isn't faint-hearted work, Cook says. Sometimes you have to navigate sheer mountain cliffs or deep gullies where rattlesnakes like to nest: "It is hot and dirty work. Lots of times you're putting the trail back in order by removing blown-down trees."

Sometimes thunderstorms blow in and drench your only dry clothes—or radios, the only contact to the outside world. There can be injuries and occasional accidents, too. Once he saw a loaded packhorse spook, stumble, and fall over the edge of a trail.

One time he was hiking with another volunteer when she was injured: "She was about two hundred feet in front of me on the trail, when suddenly she whirled around, grabbed my arm, wild-eyed and said, 'Vern, why did you do that?' She thought I'd thrown a rock at her. But it turned out her arm had been struck by a heavy rock that was dislodged from the crag above her by a bighorn sheep. She was bleeding pretty heavily."

Fortunately, Cook knew how to bandage and treat her arm, which still bears the scar.

Typically, the volunteering stints go off without any injuries, and the volunteers form tight communities and are treated to amazing natural splendor: "You see rainbow trout and salmon flashing in the clearest mountain streams. Once I saw a black bear with triplets."

One night after supper on an Oregon trip, Cathy Conover, a U.S. Forest Service staff person who first convinced Cook to start leading wilderness volunteer trips, said she had something to show him. She led the way to the top of a two-thousand-foot abyss. Below was the dark forest, in the distance, the setting sun on the Eagle Cap Range of the Willowa Mountains. "That was an inspiring moment," Cook says. "And why I do this work."

CHAPTER SEVEN

Spread the Prosperity

Invest in Entrepreneurs

"The energy, money and brainpower being devoted to the practice of lending to the world's poor is unprecedented. 'Previously if we screamed, people didn't listen. Now, if we whisper, the whole world will hear,'" says Mohammed Yunus, who shares the Nobel Peace Prize with his Grameen Bank.

—Business Week

The rising up of determined entrepreneurs and would-be capitalists, many of whom have never had a savings account, is one of the most exciting, satisfying aspects of the give-back solution. Many of these first-time business owners are women, who traditionally have done unpaid, backbreaking work, carrying heavy loads of firewood or walking miles for plastic containers of water.

Any money they managed to scrape together was handed over to partners, husbands, and relatives. Or it was hidden under mattresses or rugs in mud huts to save for the next emergency, maybe a funeral or a sick child, common occurrences in their disease-heavy world.

But thankfully, with the explosion of women's empowerment programs, microfinance and patient capital investments, and other entrepreneurial programs, the financial fortunes of women and men all over the world are shifting dramatically.

Microfinance: A Proven Way Out of Poverty

Microfinance involves extending a small loan, often from fifty dollars to one hundred fifty dollars, plus business guidance, help with savings accounts, insurance, and other support, so microentrepreneurs can invest in things like weaving looms, goats, sewing machines, mobile phones, and charcoal to jump-start small start-up businesses. Thousands of microfinance institutions offer you the opportunity to be a banker to people living in poverty. After you extend a loan or grant, you often hear how your recipient is doing and how their business is faring, and when your loan is repaid, you can choose to invest in another enterprise, anywhere you like.

Helping people help themselves has never been easier—or more rewarding. You can journey to villages and help budding start-ups, from market stalls selling vegetables to communities' first laundromats, gain traction and find markets. Or you can support microfinance efforts right where you are through organizations such as Acumen Fund, a nonprofit global venture fund that invests in developing-world enterprises—like a thriving malaria-bed-net factory—that deliver health care, water, housing, and employment to impoverished people, including tens of thousands of Kenyans.

The ripple effect of this kind of small investment is huge, because microfinance borrowers are usually people like Priscilla, a young mother living in a poor village in Ghana.

Priscilla sailed through business-education programs

"The rise of microcredit has brought many small loans to people in poor countries and rural areas who had no access to traditional banks or could not present the kind of bona fides a bank requires. Microcredit has sparked a revolution in the international development community, proving the existence of plenty of credit-worthy people who are simply overlooked by traditional banks."

—Ode Magazine

sponsored by Freedom from Hunger, which also helped her get small loans for her charcoal business and open her first-ever savings account. Now Priscilla can finally invest in herself and her children. "Before, my children could only sit at the gate of the school. Now they go in," Priscilla says.

I hear over and over from those who work routinely in the developing world that people there are more determined, resourceful, and hopeful than we can even imagine. They have to be to have survived all they have: famine, genocide, disease, prejudice, and more. Many of them start working at 4:00 a.m.—or earlier—and don't stop until long after dark, feeding and raising children in between. I saw it for myself in Africa and Thailand. Proud women, bundled up in jackets and caps, rode into town on motor scooters before dawn, sometimes with children in their laps and on the back of the scooter, to put up modest vegetable stands. These people aren't asking for a handout, but for a hand up, and that's where we can step in.

Acumen Fund's Jacqueline Novogratz told me about Charles, a man she witnessed in the postelection violence in Kenya in 2007. In her twenty-five years of work in the developing world, Novogratz has seen many wrenching scenes, but stepping into the slums of Kiberia, Kenya—into the Toi Market—staggered her. This marketplace had always captured the best of Kenya's entrepreneurship and vitality, color, and hope, she said. Each of the three thousand stalls in the market once represented "a chance for upward mobility," she said. "What I saw really kicked me in the gut in a way I wasn't prepared for. Everything was completely burnt and razed to the ground.

"But then I saw a man still putting up makeshift tables to sell beautifully washed and pressed baby clothes, hoping against hope. I said, 'Who will buy this?' And he looked at me with tears in his eyes and said, 'I have to hope, because they have taken everything else.'"

That man was Charles Onyango, who had started out with nothing a few years before but used microfinance loans and his own determination to expand his business selling children's clothing in three stalls. He could then afford to put his children in good schools. "He lost his entire life's savings in the fires of a single night," Novogratz said.

Joseph Campbell said that when you're on your path, the universe rises up to meet you. If enterprising people like Charles are working hard to place themselves on the path of productivity and prosperity, what a privilege to meet them with ideas, encouragement, pragmatic solutions—and investments.

If you want to go and do some heavy lifting of business ventures in the developing world by heading overseas—or lift them up right where you are—here's a host of ways you can help launch economic development around the world. We all can do something with our time, talents, and travel to make the world more prosperous and equitable for all.

Here's Your Challenge: Almost Half of the World's People Live on Less than Two Dollars a Day

So says the World Bank.

Twenty-five percent of the world's people receive 75 percent of the world's income. Meanwhile, about 80 percent of the working poor—about four hundred million families—have no access to microfinance services, says microfinance leader Unitus. How might their economic well-being—and the entire world—be transformed if many of these individuals who want to work can receive a job, a small loan, or a grant? Most of the world's people don't want to depend on charity. They want to work and find a way to be productive and make a sustainable living. But they're often denied loans, because they have no credit, or are given loans with such high interest rates they can't repay them.

ONE TARGET TO SHOOT FOR

More than two thousand delegates from more than 110 countries attended the Global Microcredit Summit in 2006 in Canada. They set the goal of ensuring that 175 million of the world's poorest families, especially the women of these families, receive credit for self-employment and other financial and business services by the end of 2015. If you've ever struggled financially, you know what a light it can be when someone gives you the smallest boost. How cool would it be to be that spark of hope for someone with a dream?

Here's Your Opportunity

HELP BUDDING ENTREPRENEURS OPEN SAVINGS ACCOUNTS AND SUSTAIN FIRST BUSINESSES

Global Volunteers: Go to South Africa and help assist professionals with capacity building in these areas:

- Catering: A women's cooperative that cooks for schools, community weddings, funerals, and local gatherings needs training on small business management and marketing.
- Baking: A women's group, equipped with two industrial ovens and mixers, needs electricians to complete the wiring to put its bakery into production. Then volunteers can work with the bakers on project management and marketing.
- Brick making: Volunteers can train young adults in logistics planning and produce improvement and procurement.

- Poultry farming: Volunteers are needed to help teach local women marketing and fund-raising strategies as well as practices for maximizing poultry growth and feeding. www.globalvolunteers.org

❧ **United Planet:** Guatemala is a highly patriarchal society plagued by alcohol, poverty, and domestic violence. United Planet is working to turn the situation around for some of the women and their children. Partnering with a local shelter, it has created a laundromat to help battered women regain control of their lives and achieve some economic independence. Volunteers are needed to assist with the implementation of the laundromat's business plan, including the budget and marketing, training of women and shelter staff on operation and planning, and teaching of basic English and Spanish reading and writing. www.unitedplanet.com

❧ **Global Volunteer Network:** Help women from the red-light district in Kolkata, India, learn computer and business skills as they form their own businesses. Volunteers with Web design, photography, or jewelry-making skills are needed to work with women in the fair-trade market. www.volunteer.org.nz

❧ **ProWorld:** Support microbusinesses in Thailand, or work with Peruvian people to launch and maintain everything from bee-keeping operations to guinea-pig-breeding businesses. You can also choose to help rural Peruvian women, some of whom are escaping abusive situations, take steps toward independence by learning ceramics, knitting, candle making, and other crafts, which are sold at local markets. www.myproworld.org

&o **Village Volunteers:** Assist local women in business development. You may work with artisans working in pottery, sewing, baking, or textiles in rural villages in Kenya, Ghana, India, or Nepal. Volunteers may also work on local research projects, work with traditional healers, musicians, or artisans, or document oral accounts to capture and preserve cultural and family history for orphans. www.villagevolunteers.org

&o **Global Citizens Network:** In Brazil, help women who have a long history of weaving palm fronds into bags, mats, and hats on business development to increase their earnings and develop a co-op building that will serve as a meeting place. Help develop and support a community center in Tanzania that will provide training classes, promote small-scale economic initiatives, and offer work space for women's businesses. www. globalcitizens.org

&o **Volunteer Kenya:** Provide basic business skills to microenterprise groups, creating income-generating businesses like sewing and tailoring shops, bee-keeping operations, horticultural projects, and fish ponds for harvesting and selling fish. You'll give training seminars on accounting/bookkeeping, pricing, competition, business planning, cost-benefit analysis, marketing, and other business topics. www.volunteerkenya.org

✺ **World Endeavors:** Empower indigenous Guatemalan women, often struggling with poverty, alcoholism, and depression. You'll help them learn tools and seize opportunities to improve themselves. Working with social workers, you can provide workshops on topics ranging form women's rights to handicrafts to economic development. www.worldendeavors.org

One Volunteer's Journey: Helping Launch Green Businesses

Arnab Banerjee volunteered with a ProWorld project in Peru, where he helped local people in Chicon launch an ecotourism project: "This was probably the most interesting and satisfying job I ever had, and it was based in one of the most beautiful places I have ever visited! I worked with two other volunteers, and our job was to work with a group of young people in Chicon to help set up an ecotourism project in the Chicon Valley. The aim of the project was to stop the people of Chicon from destroying local forests and encourage them to look after the forests instead by providing them with an alternative source of income utilizing the forests. Our job involved teaching English, computing, basic management skills, and finance, helping to clear the tracks (which meant machete-ing our way through forests!), creating a website, and designing leaflets. The work was extremely varied and really rewarding, as you could see your work make a real difference."

❧ **Global Service Corps:** Work with rural Tanzanian farming communities affected by HIV/AIDS to increase their crop yields and learn sustainable, organic farming methods. www.globalservicecorps.org

❧ **Cross-Cultural Solutions:** Volunteers with skills and experience in business, management, accounting, law, grant writing, information technology, marketing, fund-raising, counseling, psychology, social work, and other skills can help small, African, female-owned businesses, including restaurants, grocery stores, poultry keeping, market stalls, catering, batik making, and handicrafts. Volunteers may pitch in to help set up and navigate new computer systems, teach basic accounting and organizational skills, practice conversational English with the women, and brainstorm and share ideas about fund-raising, income-generating activities, marketing, etc. Volunteers may also help produce products such as jewelry, batiks, and handicrafts. www.crossculturalsolutions.org

QUESTIONS TO ASK
- How proactive will I need to be at my project?
- Do the business owners already have a business plan—or is this a start-up in the early stages?
- Will I largely be involved with listening and information gathering to assess their needs? Does the enterprise have a market?
- Should I bring any business or office supplies?
- I have no business background but really want to dive and help. What can I do?

- Can you tell me more about the enterprise, co-op, women's group, etc., with which I'll be working?
- How is the women's physical and emotional health?
- What do they hope to accomplish?
- What are some of the obstacles in their community, from domestic abuse to ongoing military conflict to illiteracy to everyday challenges with meeting basic needs for water and food?

One Success Story: Acumen Fund

This nonprofit global venture fund that uses entrepreneurial approaches to solve the problems of global poverty is one organization to watch—and engage with. Acumen has invested in businesses powered by hardworking people in Africa and Asia that deliver clean water, irrigation systems, new homes, and energy to those around them. More than fifty million receive critical goods and services from businesses like Water Health International and IDE India, which serves the estimated 750 million Indians who have no access to water. "That is a stark challenge to the world. But it's also time for the world to see that the poor are not just passive recipients of charity but are full individuals with the desire and potential to participate," says Jacqueline Novogratz, who founded Acumen Fund in 2001.

Another success story is celebrated in Tanzania. In 2002, Acumen gave a $325,000 loan to a small venture, A to Z Textile Mills, to make anti-malaria bed nets to protect people from malaria-bearing mosquitoes at night. The company paid off its loan four years later and now employs thousands of people, largely women. "This little factory that didn't exist before now provides protection for twenty million people. It's so mind-boggling, unimaginable. To come into a factory with seven thousand people working is just not something I ever imagined we'd be able to do. But that now changes the prism of what's possible," says Novogratz.

Novogratz was an idealist from an early age, wondering what was possible. Then, in her twenties, she was working for the international loan division of Chase, traveling to forty countries in three years, and her world pivoted toward those living in poverty when she saw millions of loans going to wealthy people. Who, she wondered, was helping the poor access such financing for their ventures?

At twenty-five, she went to Rwanda on a microfinance project and helped a group of women making beignets, batonnets, samosas, and other baked goods launch their failing business. The women—Marie-Rose, Gaudence, Josepha, Immaculata, Prudence, Consolatea, and others—were not only not making money; they were losing it. "Money—income—is fundamental to any conversation about women's rights, reproductive health, equality, you name it. Money is the starting point," says Novogratz.

In six months, Novogratz helped the women expand and grow and maintain their business. She began to dream more about what could be done in Africa if larger factories could employ large numbers of people and spark large opportunities.

In the Rwandan genocide in the 1990s, nearly all the women in the bakery perished. In a *Stanford Business Magazine* article, Novogratz explained, "Women played out every role of the genocide: witness, bystander, victim, and perpetrator. It underscores for me why systems are so critical not only to economic development, but ultimately, to peace."

For more info: www.acumenfund.org

FROM COFFEE-TABLE DREAMS TO COMMERCIAL SUCCESS: WHAT VOLUNTEERS CAN DO

A Cross-Cultural Solutions project launched five years ago by a group of Costa Rican women eager for an alternative way of living illustrates how volunteers can help launch new businesses. A group of women in Santa Clara, San Carlos, wanted to earn some money for their families and develop their own creativity. They took a class at the Instituto Tecnológico (TEC), a national university located in Santa Clara, about recycling processes.

An idea caught their attention, and they decided to try it out themselves: recycling paper for arts and crafts projects. Since they all had family duties, they met at their own homes, often around a coffee table, having no structure or clear idea of what to do with their ambitions and knowledge.

Around that time, they asked for CCS volunteers, who helped them develop a plan for their business. Volunteers helped them get organized, improve the quality of their product, and create new designs. Others taught them marketing strategies and sales skills.

At the beginning, the women learned how to make paper, but later, with the help of CCS volunteers, they started to create arts and crafts. For instance, a CCS volunteer who was an artist taught them how to paint. Even after volunteers went home, the women continued to develop their talent, and now their products are beautifully decorated.

Other volunteers returned to help them with financial information, bookkeeping, and business management. Some volunteers helped make paper, bead necklaces, paint, pack products, and help at the store. Others focused on advertising and marketing in the community.

> "I know that I alone cannot change the world, but with the help of friends, we can make an impact."
>
> —Dan Weiss,
> founder of Amizade

The women say that the strong and permanent presence of CCS volunteers during the past five years has greatly helped them launch their organization. Martha, one of the members, says that volunteers have helped them better understand their targeted costumer group.

"The women have also said that this project has given them a focus in life, made them less economically reliant on their husbands, and dramatically improved their self-esteem," says Anthony LaFrisco, Jr., CCS communications manager.

If this volunteer project calls to you, volunteers now are working to teach the women English so they can better serve potential customers.

What Volunteers Can Really Accomplish: Amizade

When you're dripping in the sun, straining to lift one more brick onto the foundation of a new school, or when you're struggling to convey a money matter to first-time business owners, it's easy to wonder if what you're doing really matters. In those moments, try to step back. Then think of your efforts merging with a long line of volunteers who came before you and will pick up when you go home.

And think of this project and legions like it, which show what kind of transformations really can happen when volunteers fall in love with a community and stay for the long haul.

In the middle of the tropical forest, on the confluence of the Tapajos and Amazon rivers in Brazil, sits Santarem, a city of more than three hundred thousand. Its people are much poorer than other Brazilians. Almost half of the population lives on less than one dollar day.

Inadequate housing, poor health and nutrition, and failing educational systems are all prevalent in Santarem and in the surrounding countryside. To exacerbate the existing poverty, in recent years, several large multinational agribusiness companies have begun to clear-cut the region and grow soy and rice, which is dramatically changing the existing ecosystems and having major environmental impacts.

Back in 1992, Dan Weiss was volunteering in Santerem and saw the poverty around him, including fragile straw huts that fell apart during the rainy season. He felt called to create his own organization: Amizade, which is Portuguese for "friendship."

With the help of his friends, including all the new ones in Brazil, Weiss's organization went on to help a community that could have gone unnoticed. Take heart in a project like this when you wonder what you're really accomplishing.

Since 1994, Amizade and local volunteers in Santerem have helped lift up the community through a variety of income-generation, education, health, and other projects. It has:

- Built a vocational training center for street children—the center's taught carpentry, sewing, silk screening, and electronics to over nine hundred teenagers.
- Built a children's health clinic—now, a community of twenty-five thousand people has access to prenatal and early childhood health care.
- Renovated a kitchen for a program working with street children, which allowed Amizade to go from

feeding two hundred children to over nine hundred children per day.

- Built a well-drilling center, which brings fresh water to communities and schools—volunteers have also drilled a half a dozen wells, bringing fresh water to hundreds of people in isolated communities.
- Built an orthopedic workshop—now, a city of 250,000 people has access to affordable orthopedic shoes; additionally, the workshop employs ten developmentally disabled teenagers.
- Built a small hotel for a program that works with handicapped teenagers and adults—the hotel serves as a vocational training program and also generates income for the program.
- Built additional classrooms for schools and community organizations serving over one thousand kids.

For more info: www.amizade.org

Helping Out from Home

If you want to be an agent from your own home or office and still make a meaningful connection with a promising entrepreneur, look no further than the Internet. Log on and help jump-start the visions of enterprising cobblers, sheepherders, seamstresses, and others reaching for greater prosperity around the world.

Got a spare $100? $50? Through a microfinance organization, you can offer it to a business owner living on two dollars or less a day. Then, sit back and enjoy the satisfaction of watching your investments take hold. You can get a real sense of just how far a small investment can ripple out and change the trajectory of someone's life. Does it get any better than that?

One Volunteer's Journey: Granting New Business Wishes

Mike Messina, a Des Moines, Iowa, paralegal is a perfect example of what can be done—right where you are. He's proof that the saying "If you give a guy a fish, he's going to eat for a day, but if you give him a net, he can feed himself for a lifetime" isn't just a worn, tired adage. It sprang to life for Messina when his world collided with that of a Samoan woman.

Thirty-six-year-old Amelia Sagato fishes for a living, selling some of her fish at the local market, as well as in front of her village road so passing traffic can easily see her catch. On a good day, Amelia can earn the equivalent of $40, and her income helps send her six children to school and keep her family afloat.

Sagato uploaded her wishes on the website of Kiva, a microfinance organization (www.kiva.org). She said she wished for small loans to buy fishing nets, spears, and baskets to store and carry her catch to market. Her hopes called to Messina. He decided to loan her $250. So far, she has repaid $187 of the loan, and her business is prospering.

Messina got inspired to explore microfinance in 2000 when he read *American Dreamer,* a book about Henry

Wallace. "While Wallace was vice-president during World War II, he tried to convince President Roosevelt that the only way to win the postwar peace was to declare a century of the common man, led by the United States, to eradicate poverty. Had Wallace been nominated for a second term as vice-president instead of Truman, I think we would be looking at a different world today."

Messina also heard about the work of Grameen Bank's Mohammed Yunus, a microfinance pioneer, who, along with his bank, was awarded the Nobel Peace Prize in 2006. For thirty years, Yunus's bank has extended loans to more than seven million poor people, 97 percent of whom are women, in seventy-three thousand villages in Bangladesh. By 2010, Grameen hopes to reach 100 percent of the poor families in Bangladesh with microfinance.

When he heard about the microfinance organization Kiva on a *60 Minutes* segment, Messina acted. Working with Kiva, he's loaned at least $2,200 to forty-six business people in the developing world, including a Lebanese barber, Afghani and Ugandan shop owners, and a Bolivian leather maker named Juan Carlos Jimenez: "He buys cattle hides, makes leather, and then sells the leather to other artisans, who use them to make things like shoes, jackets, and suitcases. I was able to loan Juan Carlos $125, which was fully repaid. In addition to working with leather, he also studies biochemistry at a nearby university. How cool is that?"

None of Messina's loans have been defaulted on. He

enjoys the dignified way that Kiva allows people like him, "who have a little extra cash from time to time," provide operating capital for entrepreneurs in the developing world. "I can't think of a better use of the Internet," he says.

Messina would like to see loans going into all the hot spots in the world:

"The more connected we are with people around the world, the less likely we will want to go to war with them. I think we can do a lot more good with our capital than we can with bombs."

Kiva's recipients show, every day, just how far a modest loan goes in their world. A small study in Bangladesh found that 48 percent of the poorest households with access to a microloan rose above the poverty level.

Kiva and other organizations have also mined a rich, give-back vein among Americans wanting to lift up the desires of hardworking, determined people. Only three years old, it has loaned more than $19 million to about thirty thousand small businesses in thirty-nine countries. Their loan-repayment rate? About 99.8 percent.

A MOMENT WITH MOHAMMED YUNUS: THE ORIGINAL BANKER TO THE POOR

My friend Tana Myers was spearheading a fabulous conference in Denver just as I was on deadline for this project. It featured social business and microeconomic development opportunities for young people. I didn't think I could lift my head from the keyboard, but Tana and our mutual friend Katie Hoffner showed me otherwise. I was trying to avoid the phone, but one morning, I answered it. I am glad I did. "Can you come—like by 1:30?" Katie asked. "Tana wanted me to call you. Mohammed Yunus has an opening in his schedule!"

With just $27, Yunus made small loans to Bangladesh borrowers in 1976. Now Grameen Bank has given about $6.7 billion to 7.5 million borrowers. He's a rock star, and not just in the give-back world. I made it to Denver, one hour away, in record time. I found out I only had ten minutes for my interview, which quickly morphed from my "interview with Mohammed" to my "moment with Mohammed." But this is one charismatic man who doesn't need much time to be inspiring.

What lingers with me most was his response when I asked him why so many of us are drawn to giving back right now. His answer, not surprisingly, was intriguing: we've lived with a restricted, narrow interpretation of what it truly means to be human, and giving back is liberating us to discover our true, more giving natures. "You've been with the theory that people are money-making machines. That money is a means to an end. But human beings are not money-making machines. They can't express themselves fully that way. So you are stepping out and expressing yourself more and discovering your enduring natures...Since you are true human beings, you are trying to break open your doors to express yourselves," he smiled.

BE A BANKER TO THE POOR: INVEST IN ENTREPRENEURS

If you want to help resourceful, resilient people build a new life and

"African women—among the poorest on earth—don't want handouts. They want a chance to change their own lives. Most of them have their own businesses; actually most have two or three. They earn income, even if it's only a dollar a day. They bear and care for children, send them to school, cook, and clean. When one of their own children dies, the others pool their money to pay for a funeral. Every day they have to make decisions between bad and terrible alternatives. The mutual support is powerful, because every woman understands how weak she is alone. But still they dance. It is to this spirit, this audacity that exists in people across the world to whom we owe the chance to make their own lives better. And maybe the rest of us will learn to dance a little better along the way."

—*Jacqueline Novogratz,*
Acumen Fund

employment, there are many organizations through which you can engage. There's no shortage of organizations to contact if extending a small loan and/or grant to a business person in the developing world appeals to you. Here are a few to check out:

Accion International: This giant in the microfinance world's been offering microenterprise loans, business training, technical assistance, financing, and support for entrepreneurs working their way out of poverty since 1961. It helps men and women entrepreneurs in twenty-five countries. www.accion.org

GlobalGiving: The *Washington Post* has described this organization as "foreign aid at the speed of light." Ex-World Bankers Dennis Whittle and Mari Kuraishi created GlobalGiving to be the "eBay for international philanthropy." When you visit this site, you can browse through more than four hundred projects, some of which are microfinance-related, and contribute any amount you wish. You'll also receive an update on your donation. www.globalgiving.org

❦ **FINCA International:** FINCA International founder John Hatch developed the village banking method. Donations to FINCA can be designated to a specific program as loan capital. www.villagebanking.org

❦ **Opportunity International:** Help provide savings accounts and low-cost life and farming insurance in developing countries. www.opportunity.org

❦ **Unitus:** Started in 2001, Unitus says it's empowered over 2.4 million microentrepreneurs throughout Asia, Africa, and Latin America and hopes to reach fifteen million families by 2010. www.unitus.com

Mery Mejía, from Barranquilla, Colombia, is a client of Accion partner Fundación Mario Santo Domingo, and Accion shares her story to show what can be done.

Meet a Colombian Microentrepreneur

Until Mejia and her family became *desplazados*—displaced by the violence in the mountains of Colombia—they had been getting by on the income from her husband's job in the fields. But when paramilitaries began to heavily recruit her husband and threaten her family, they began to get worried. Mejia and her husband, Manuel, refused to join the paramilitaries or to pay the taxes they demanded, so she and her three children were forced to flee. In 2001, Mejia arrived in Barranquilla on foot after a four-day journey. "We came with nothing. I suffered a lot. I cried and cried," she remembers.

After searching high and low for work, she came across a man from her town who now owns a restaurant in Barranquilla. He hired her and paid her thirty thousand pesos a week (or fourteen U.S. dollars). She also discovered a local program in Barranquilla that would allow her to set up a four-by-four-meter hut for her family on some land outside of the city. The hut had a plastic roof and a basic cement floor but no gas or electricity. The neighborhood was unsafe, and Mejia continued to search for a way to feed and protect her children.

Through friends she found out about Accion partner Fundación Mario Santo Domingo and was able to get a loan to buy industrial ovens, mixers, pans, trays, raw materials, and ingredients to make bread. She had little experience making bread but was determined to make the business work and took Accion's ABCs of Business to learn more about running a business. The course provided Mejia with practical tools that have served her well. The ABCs of Business units that she took provided recipes for various kinds of bread and specific instructions for pricing them. In addition, Mejia learned the importance of establishing a brand, setting reliable hours, and carefully tracking earnings and expenses. Mejia proudly shows off her ledger, revealing carefully kept notes on sales, income, and expenses, formatted just as the ABCs of Business curriculum instructs.

Mejia now runs a small bread shop called MaryPan, which is enabling her to repay her loan, cover her rent, and feed her family. She works hard, cooking all night and sleeping briefly at midday. With her next loan, she plans to buy a mixer to make sweet dessert breads. Her family lives together in one room behind the bakery she is renting. It is an improvement from their living situation just a few years ago, but it gets uncomfortably hot near the ovens and is still tight quarters. Mejia says she will continue to work toward her dream of owning a home someday where she and her family can live comfortably.

For more info: www.accion.org

ASSIST IN BUILDING ENTREPRENEUR INFRASTRUCTURE

If you want to help social entrepreneurs and businesses thrive right where you are, here are a couple of inspiring organizations that can open some doors for your engagement. And again, search the microfinance and social business listings on websites, such as www.globalgiving.org and www.networkforgood.org.

Pump Aid: Clean water is flowing for school children and their families in southern Africa through this organization's innovative Elephant Pump, based on a two-thousand-year-old

Chinese design. The pumps were tested in Zimbabwe and are durable and maintained by local people. You can contribute to this project and also enjoy its lesson plans and other information about the communities in which it operates. www.pumpaid.org

❧ **KickStart:** KickStart sells inexpensive technologies, like human-powered irrigation pumps, to farmers in impoverished communities in Africa. The technologies dramatically boost the farmer's ability to move from subsistence farming to commercial, irrigated farming. The organization says that since 1991, it has helped sixty thousand families start businesses that together generate more than $65 million in new profits and wages each year. It's helped nearly three hundred thousand people out of poverty. Kick Start was started by Martin Fisher, who has spent much of his career living in Africa and is a strong advocate for empowering impoverished people through earned income and economic opportunity. www.kickstart.org

Helping in the United States: Boost Employment Here

To help people get and keep jobs here, go to the Idealist website, www.idealist.org, and search for volunteering opportunities in your own state under the search word "jobs." You'll discover tons of opportunities to help people in your area find employment. You can become a job mentor, employment/interview coach, help fill out job applications, solve workplace questions, or pitch in in some other way to help people, from at-risk youths to recent immigrants to older individuals, become employed in your community.

Here's just one volunteering opportunity that popped up on Idealist's site:

❦ **People Helping People:** PHP is a Salt Lake City–based mentorship program that helps low-income families and single moms develop the self-confidence, tools, networks, and resources to create a better future for themselves and their children through employment. www.phputah.org

Check out what you can do in your community to take a bite out of unemployment and help others find the work they deserve. Here are some other opportunities that boost employment in the United States:

❦ **Career Gear:** Offer your volunteer time to help provide business clothing, interview coaching, and job-retention services so more men get and keep jobs. Career Gear has affiliates in New York City, Boston, Miami, Houston, New Haven, and Washington, D.C. www.careergear.org

❦ **AARP:** This nationwide powerhouse has volunteering opportunities to help people become or stay financially stable and find jobs. See if your state has an AARP money-management program you could volunteer with, and feel the satisfaction of helping older or disabled Americans who have difficulty budgeting, paying routine bills, or keeping track of financial matters. www.aarp.org

※ **Homeboy Industries:** This cool program reaches out to at-risk and formerly gang-involved youth and offers job placement, training, and education. It started in one of the toughest neighborhoods in Los Angeles twenty years ago and is now a national model. Homeboy Industries now employs young people to run a silk-screening business that makes custom T-shirts and other clothing. Homeboy Bakery and Homegirl Café are among other enterprises. www.homeboy-industries.org

※ **Dress for Success:** Join forces with this nonprofit that helps low-income women achieve success in their careers and lives by providing professional attire, professional and emotional support, and career-development tools. With a focus on the importance of women's economic independence, Dress for Success also created the Professional Women's Group Program and Career Center, which offers ongoing support and career guidance. www.dressforsuccess.org

CHAPTER EIGHT

Ease Conflicts

Be the Peace You Want to See in the World

"Out beyond ideas of wrongdoing and right doing, there is a field. I'll meet you there."

—*Rumi*

When villages are torn apart by conflict, malaria nets don't cover babies' beds, women can't sustain new businesses, supplies don't reach medical clinics, and children don't cross the thresholds of schools. When regions are at war, humanitarian progress vanishes.

A world that works for everyone is a peaceful world. And we all play a part in whether the world becomes more peaceful—or not. As I wrote in my last book, *Peace in Our Lifetime*, it's come down to us. This is our time to make things right. This is our time to stand up and use our true power to be instruments for peace in our own lives and in the world.

It's how we find the healthy, peaceful families, communities, and nations for which we long. It's how we move from a war consciousness to a peace consciousness. "Nobody is going to do it for us," says Arn Chorn Pond, a Vietnamese refugee turned peacemaker whose entire family was killed in Vietnam in 1975. "You and I have to make choices every step we go in our life."

Every volunteer opportunity is an opportunity to create greater peace, when we discover how much we have in common and bring people together in more stable communities. It's almost not right to carve out a separate chapter for peace-related volunteering projects, since every act of service anchors in a more cooperative world. Every hour you give back will make the world instantly a better place. And every volunteer is a peacemaker in his or her own right.

Yet if you want to focus your time, talents, and travel on creating a culture of peace through some groups specifically engaged in that endeavor, there are many rich options. Like all forms of giving back, the number of people and organizations easing hostilities, reconciling differences, and building peaceful communities is surging.

They're carving out peace through every means imaginable: by listening, playing, forgiving, negotiating, talking, rebuilding, finding common ground, and dining together to reach a higher plane. And many of their efforts have been accelerated by ordinary volunteers.

Are you drawn to helping people reach for something greater than chronic fighting, especially those living in conflict, often for generations? Do you have a sense of what this kind of service work might look like for you? Do you want to help refugees heal from the trauma of war or help people worn down by fighting learn to reconcile—or at least listen to one another with a less judgmental heart? Or maybe you like the idea of helping young people, more open to letting down their bitterness, come together in play and sports—a growing part of peace work around the world.

From Bosnia to the West Bank, you can help these and others reach for that something greater. Like all the volunteer options, it's just finding the right match for your desires.

Here's Your Challenge: Military Campaigns And Conflict Rock Far Too Much Of The World

Half of the children who don't attend school live in countries touched by conflict, according to Teachers Without Borders

ONE TARGET TO SHOOT FOR

According to experts at Oxford University, genocide and violent conflicts are down worldwide. Despite the violence you see in the media, military conflicts are actually waning. More people on the Earth are at peace than at war—something to inspire hope, for sure. What if we committed to keeping the peace, right where we are? What if we decided that whether the world continues this upward, hopeful trend—or not—depends on our actions? One goal to shoot for: begin by making your own piece of the world more peaceful—and then reach out and help reconciliation ripple out elsewhere.

Here's Your Opportunity

ENGAGE AROUND PEACEMAKING AND CONFLICT RESOLUTION

This is a very fluid area of volunteering, so keep checking out new opportunities on the volunteer-vacation sites and others like www.idealist.org and www.worldvolunteerweb.org.

Global Volunteer Network: Help Liberians at the Buduburam Refugee Settlement in Ghana, who've been ravaged by civil war for years, continue to enjoy greater peace and reconciliation. The organization you'll work with was founded by Liberian refugees who saw the need and potential for peace among their people. You'll conduct tribal leaders reconciliation forums, workshops, and peace-education classes; train community peace-cell leaders; teach conflict resolution; and help train refugee mothers in life and child-rearing skills as well as micro-business management. www.volunteer.org.nz

Volunteers for Peace: In northern Uganda, people have been forced out of their homes during the conflict between the Lords Resistance Army and the Ugandan government. Through this volunteer work camp, you can help young, displaced people affected by war regain their lives and work together on community service projects. You can also help members of the community use democratic tools to promote peace in the region and help construct a youth center for the community. www.vfp.org

   Global Youth Connect: Millions of Iraqis have been up-
rooted and forced to flee their homes during the Iraq War. At
least 750,000 of these refugees have settled in Jordan. Youth
are invited to join Global Youth Connect and partner organizations to volunteer for the Iraqi Refugee Solidarity Initiative. The initiative is joining young people from the United
States, Iraq, and Jordan to understand the root causes of the
crisis and identify ways to address the situation, among other
things. www.globalyouthconnect.org

One Organization that Heals with a Simple Tool: Compassionate Listening

"Violence is the language of the unheard," Dr. Martin
Luther King, Jr., said. Peacemaker Thich Nhat Hanh said,
"If we could read the secret history of our enemies, we
should find in each person's life sorrow and suffering
enough to disarm all hostility."

The laying on of ears can counter hate and mistrust
and calm even the most violent confrontation. And compassionate listening—an everyday tool that anyone can
use to ease conflicts—is a form of humanitarian aid,
finds Compassionate Listening, a groundbreaking organization working in the Middle East and other regions.

Compassionate Listening has trained more than 5,500
people in twenty-four U.S. states, as well as Canada, the
Middle East, and Europe in compassionate listening.
These trained listeners then go as delegations to volunteer to listen for peace building and reconciliation.

More than five hundred U.S. citizens have participated in twenty-two training delegations in the Middle East since 1990. Other retreats have been held between descendents of those who died in the Holocaust and descendents of German soldiers. Many people practice compassionate listening to ease tensions and heal traumas in their own U.S. communities (see One Volunteer's Journey, p. 188).

If you're trained by this organization, you'll learn how to listen without judging, correcting, debating, defending, or trying to fix anything. "You listen to someone's story with an open heart, creating a loving space whether you like what they're saying or not," says Compassionate Listening founder Leah Green.

Compassionate Listening's curriculum was developed after ten years of work on the ground with Israelis and Palestinians. And it's informed, as well, by Green's own sensibilities and experiences. In 1979, she was watching a sunset in Jerusalem when a man walked toward her, coming from the direction of a nearby Arab village. She reacted in fear, even though the man was warm and smiling. Green ran away, afraid she was in danger. Though she'd always prided herself on being open-minded and accepting, Green started to ask herself some tough questions. How, she wondered, could she be so afraid of people she didn't even know?

She knew she wanted to hear others' stories, to defuse prejudices and tension, and in 1997 she created the

Compassionate Listening Project, now known as Compassionate Listening.

"Compassionate listening helps people bridge what can seem like gaping, insurmountable distances," Green says. "It softens people's hearts and helps them be more willing to stretch for peace.

"During one of our delegations, we met with and listened to the governor of Gaza. He was very official and diplomatic and gave us lots of information. He also described daily humiliations, like having to cross the checkpoints in front of the Israeli soldiers."

As the man shared his story, he kept it in an intellectual realm, "on the head level," Green remembers. But when one of the trained compassionate listeners reflected back to him the humiliation she heard in his story, he suddenly became more emotional. "His eyes teared up, and he became a different human being right in front of us. His face opened up. He got very soft. He started talking very much on the personal level about his own story. Listening from the heart, hearing people so deeply you get to their core essence, who they really are, is a very honoring experience," Green says.

Visit Compassionate Listening's website to see if there is a training session or group in your area. Or consider becoming a "Friend of Compassionate Listening" and supporting this organization.

For more info: www.compassionatelistening.org

QUESTIONS TO ASK

- What conflict or conflicts are in my project area? What is their history?
- Will I be close to any actual war zones or violence?
- Tell me about any risks.
- Do I need special skills in mediation or conflict resolution?
- Who will I be spending time with, and can you share more about their stories?

One Volunteer's Journey: Helping Hurricane Survivors

Retired educator and trained compassionate listener Barb Lehner saw the power of nonjudgmental listening in Palestine and Israel as she sat with people who'd lost everything and known far too much violence for one lifetime. But when Hurricanes Katrina and Rita hit the Gulf Coast, she went to the South and saw the massive devastation—"miles and miles of nothing," as she describes it.

She witnessed the fear and frustrations of people who'd lost their homes and belongings, who felt the government wasn't doing enough and suffered from the lack of medical services. Lehner realized her listening skills were needed much closer to home: "A group of us trained in compassionate listening got our heads together and decided to do a phone tree to listen to the stories of the survivors. It was really in my heart of hearts to do that, and it was such a cool project."

Lehner and other volunteers trained by Compassionate Listening connected with the United Methodist Church in Louisiana and piloted a program in 2006 called Care Calls USA. They started with lists of thousands of survivors and ended up offering a "listening lifeline" to about forty people in the Lake Charles area, sometimes in person, sometimes long-distance by phone.

Letting people who were feeling overwhelmed, anxious, or alone know that they weren't forgotten after all was powerful, Lehner and her team of listeners found.

"The hurricane survivors were thrilled that people would come to their area and were struck by the fact that they and people outside the region would take time out of their day to listen to them," she says. "They had such tremendous spirit and were always very quick to say, 'Well, it's been tough, but Aunt Bea or Cousin Charles is really having a harder time than me.' Their strong faith really carried them."

As did the compassionate listening. Being heard not only helped the survivors continue to be grateful to be alive—it possibly helped them stay alive: "We often heard of people who just gave up after the hurricane. Two of the people I talked with said they lost their husbands following Rita. One woman, Barbara, told me her husband wasn't able to get adequate care, and he passed away six months after the hurricane. They had lost their home and moved into a trailer, and he died from complications from a heart condition."

Lehner listened to Barbara and other family members for more than a year and a half. At one point Barbara, who also had major health problems, was hospitalized: "She was so appreciative and said she looked forward to my calls. She said, 'I know everyone has their problems and their stories here, but it just means a lot to me that you continue to call.'

"One day I called her when she was in the hospital, and her daughter answered and said, 'Oh, are you the Barb who has been calling my mom? It has made such a difference in her life!' People there really opened their doors and hearts to us, and you got so much more out of this than you gave."

Lehner believes compassionate listening can help after any crisis: "We'd be excited to share this model with others throughout the United States or world who are involved with recovery processes following disasters. All can be volunteers and do it from their own homes." Lehner is also exploring using the practice to listen to the stories of soldiers returning from the Iraq War.

"We all need a listening ear. We all need people in our lives who don't judge us and give advice, but can really connect with us. It makes such a difference in people's lives when they are truly heard," Lehner says.

Helping Out from Home

❦ **Women for Women International:** Support this organization, which has helped more than a hundred thousand women worldwide to recover, survive, and prosper in the wake of war and civil strife. The organization was founded in 1993 by Zainab Salbi, a survivor of war. It pairs American women with a "sister" from a war-ravaged country. The sisters get direct financial aid, including vocational and leadership training, microloans, and rights awareness. They also receive letters—emotional lifelines— from American women. For $27 a month, you can sponsor a woman in Afghanistan, Bosnia, Herzegovina, the Democratic Republic of Congo, Iraq, Kosovo, Nigeria, Rwanda, and Sudan. www.womenforwomen.org

PeaceWorks Foundation: Since its inception in 2002, PeaceWorks's OneVoice, a grassroots movement run by Israelis and Palestinians, has taken a bold approach to engaging these two groups in greater civic involvement. OneVoice empowers the moderate majority of Israelis and Palestinians to take a more assertive role in resolving the conflict. OneVoice works to reframe the conflict, transcending the "left vs. right" and "Israeli vs. Palestinian" paradigms and other misunderstandings that impede peace. It also uses cutting-edge technology, electronic democracy, a network of activists and member organizations, and a broad cadre of experts, dignitaries, celebrities, business leaders, and spiritual authorities. Its public negotiations process educates people about the issues themselves as well as about the art of negotiation and nonviolent conflict resolution. www.peaceworks.net

Play for Peace: Throw your support behind this awesome group, now in its eleventh year, working in Guatemala, South

Africa, India, the Middle East, and other countries. It uses play to promote relationships among people whose communities suffer from chronic cross-cultural tensions. Play for Peace teaches people to live and play together in creating more peaceful communities. www.playforpeace.org

PeacePlayers International: PeacePlayers International uses sports to unite and educate young people in divided communities. It operates on the idea that "children who play together can learn to live together." It operates in South Africa, Cyprus, the Middle East, and Ireland. www.peaceplayersintl.org

Seeds of Peace: Support this grassroots, well-respected organization. Seeds of Peace was created by the late author and journalist John Wallach after the first attack on the World Trade Center in 1993. It brings together and empowers youth from around the world to erode stereotypes and commit to understanding and reconciliation: teenagers from warring regions around the world come together at its camp in Maine or at the Seeds of Peace Center for Coexistence in Jerusalem. More than 3,500 young people from twenty-five nations have graduated from Seeds of Peace. Seeds of Peace also uses state-of-the-art technology to unite teenagers across borders. A secure listserv, SeedsNet, provides a daily forum for Seeds of Peace graduates to continue dialogue from coexistence sessions. It has become a key means of maintaining certain and secure communication during periods of unrest. It's supplemented by online coexistence sessions in a chat-room environment. www.seedsofpeace.org

Helping in the United States: Promote Peace and Conflict Resolution Here

Many people feel they can't do much to ease tensions halfway around the world—but they can sure hold a bit of the peace right where they are. They can do what they can, in their own way, to be the change they want to see in the world. Here are just a few ways you can stand up for peace in your own backyard.

  The Peace Alliance: Who isn't ready for a more peaceful nation and world? Support the Peace Alliance's efforts to build a culture of peace. This citizen-action organization supports legislation in Congress calling for a Cabinet-level Department of Peace and Nonviolence. It has inspired a grassroots movement in the United States, asking our government to address the root causes of violence and to fund and replicate programs that have proven, effective track records of reducing and preventing violence. You can volunteer to write editorials, conduct local media interviews, lobby members of Congress, organize local talks and training sessions, and meet with local leaders—from fire chiefs to school boards—to share how a Department of Peace will benefit your community. www.thepeacealliance.org

  Nonviolent Communication: This organization provides a way to get to the root of and transform conflict, violence, and pain peacefully. You can get trained in nonviolence communication and then volunteer in your own community to create practice teams, workshops, conferences, and other events. www.nonviolentcommunication.com

CHAPTER NINE

Still Other Ways to Engage

Start in Your Own Workplace

If you're somewhere on the corporate ladder or racing upward on an accelerated career track, you might assume that your dream of volunteering overseas has to be back-burnered into the future. Or you may be so buried at work that the thought of a volunteer vacation feels about as likely as early retirement.

Think again—and then again. Ten years ago, international corporate volunteering largely didn't even exist. Now it's mushrooming. At least 40 percent of major corporations support employee volunteer efforts around the world, finds the Brookings Institution's Initiative on International Volunteering and Service. What might be possible at your workplace?

If a program isn't in place, you might consider spearheading one, and you'll likely be able to rally much support in your ranks: studies find that many employees are increasingly passionate about going abroad to serve at all phases of their career.

You could begin by researching the success and workings of

other companies' service-abroad programs. Talk with other corporate volunteers about their experiences, too.

Oren Penn's story may jump-start your investigations, or at least make you want to leave your cubicle and jump on the next plane.

One Volunteer's Journey: Reaching Out to India's "Untouchables"

"My goal the past two and a half years has been to kind of relive my India experience every day," Oren Penn says.

An international tax partner for PricewaterhouseCoopers, Penn spent eight weeks on a corporate service fellowship to improve health in a remote Indian community, Orissa, one of the poorest areas of India. Through its Ulysses program, PwC sends top-performing partners to help in the developing countries in which they do business to cultivate more global leaders who are capable of solving a host of unforeseen issues.

Penn had only been married one week when he went to Orissa to work with two colleagues from the Netherlands and Mexico in the summer of 2005. Their assignment: work with the NGO Gram Vikas (which means "village development") to help grow its efforts to ease severe poverty and unsafe health conditions in Orissa's community of "untouchables," who'd been so ostracized, their health was dire.

"The untouchable are at the lowest rung of the caste system," Penn says. "We met with them in villages so remote, the people have to walk several miles to reach a water hole used for everything—cleaning clothes, going to the bathroom, drinking water. Because the water is used for every purpose and the people lack education about the dangers of doing so, the death rate is high."

Penn says that unsafe drinking water causes 80 percent of the diseases in the untouchables. The average Orrisan only lives to be fifty-six.

Gram Vikas had already created a successful, replicable model for building wells and sanitation systems to provide both irrigation and clean drinking water. The organization also had documented how the diseases and death rates dropped dramatically when their system was used. "Our task was to help them come up with ways to scale up what they were doing and reach out to more communities and villages around them," Penn says. "At first we had no idea what we were doing. We did our homework and visited all the local areas that were completely untouched by the outside world and in grave need of help."

The work felt so meaningful because he and his team members realized that the Gram Vikas model, called REACH, was so replicable that it "could really make a difference and potentially help hundreds of thousands of people over a five- to ten-year time frame," Penn says.

In the end, the team produced a written report of recommendations for the NGO and promotional materials, "off the fly and with limited computer access," to help them tell their "compelling and universal" story—and rally support from funding sources, he adds.

Penn and his colleagues helped the organization see that to scale up and be as effective as it wanted to be and become more sustainable, REACH would have to reach out to others and not try to do the work all alone. REACH also needed to teach the next generation more. Penn says: "We told them, 'You really do need to coordinate and share.'"

Gram Vikas did use the team's new promotional materials and did get additional funding to help expand its outreach. Plus, PwC has become so committed to the project, it has sent in another team to continue the work started by Penn's team. Penn will go back many times himself, since his work will also take him there. "This goes beyond social responsibility in the business sector," he says. "It opened my eyes to see more companies that care about the places in which they do business. We can make step-by-step changes by partnering with local organizations to better the health of the people living there."

Seeing people living well below poverty was overwhelming sometimes, Penn says: "We were in some communities where people felt so ignored and put down that when we first met with them, they would put out three chairs for us, and they would sit on the floor. When we sat on the floor with them, at first they didn't understand. 'Why would someone like you want to sit on our level?' they asked. "We said, 'Because we want to treat you as the human beings you are.'

"And after that, they opened up and shared, and it was really meaningful. People who were very quiet, scared, and malnourished when they came in the door were, at the end of the meeting, asking us questions like, 'What do you do for fun at home?' And we'd ask them the same questions. To actually see them laugh and enjoy themselves was more than touching. And something I keep in my head."

His advice to anyone else going to serve as he did? "Just know that if you do that, you'll get back ten times what you give, and it will show up in different ways," Penn reflects.

For instance, he said he feels his entire life now—which includes being the parent of two small children—mirrors, somehow, his time in India: "It's sort of completely changed my view of how I look at the world. I feel I've done a little bit to help a piece of the world completely ignored, I mean completely ignored, and it humbles you. It has helped open my eyes to a wide world view that I thought I shared, but I really didn't understand. I have to learn something every day. We just don't understand enough now."

Having to work as an effective team amid the challenges of Orissa has also made him a much more effective team leader now. "I've clearly taken the teaming concept as far as I possibly can every day," he says. "I've raised my game in terms of how I approach what I do."

In the meantime, he keeps a poster on his wall that he

created after his time in India to remind him every day of how he wants to walk in the world. It spells REACH.

"I wanted to come up with my own personal REACH when I came back to the United States," he says. "People are always searching for work-life balance. In my view, this is the best way to enjoy work, enhance your performance, and elevate all parts of your life as well."

You don't have to go abroad to get this kind of world view, Penn stresses, but "the more people engage in some way, the better off we'll be. And those fortunate to travel will grow as people and have a better understanding, as well, of our own country. You will get so much more meaning when you are back home."

Penn's corporate service fellowship and others like it at PricewaterhouseCoopers was set up by Building Blocks International (BBI), a nonprofit that works with multinational corporations to develop corporate service fellowships in which employees work from four weeks to a year applying their skills in community-based organizations around the world. BBI has worked with Pfizer, UPS, Cisco, and other companies. Fellows often receive their full salary during their service.

BBI CEO Jennifer Anastasoff says that more companies are deciding that they not only want to have a positive social impact around the world, but that they like to retain workers who want to change the world. Anastasoff says that 73 percent of employees involved in service through their work are more committed afterward to their jobs.

How Your Company Can Set Up a Volunteer Program

If you're developing or expanding a service program in your workplace, you might be interested in a 2007 study on the state of international corporate volunteering. In it, the Brookings Institution's Initiative on International Volunteering and Service, FSG Social Impact Advisors, and Pfizer looks at the emerging trend among thirty multinationals including Accenture, IBM, Pfizer, Starbucks, and Timberland. If your company plans to or wants to create a volunteering program, the study offers these recommendations:

- **Set goals before roles:** International corporate volunteering efforts are more successful when the business objectives have been identified in advance.

- **Walk before you run:** Corporations should first decide if they want to engage local communities where they do business or start cross-border programs. It is important to consider the company's level of experience with international programs and interest in engaging in a particular country before beginning.

- **Lead with leverage:** Opportunities to create social impact will be greater if companies leverage employees' workplace skills and knowledge.

- **Align with philanthropic and corporate social responsibility activities:** Corporate volunteer programs should serve as an extension of a company's other philanthropic initiatives, not as a separate effort.

- **Partner proactively:** Companies can save time and resources by partnering with the right organizations, such as a local NGO, to develop a volunteering program.

- **Invest in infrastructure:** Companies that establish dedicated volunteering-program management teams experience more success.

- **Communicate clearly:** Setting clear goals and explaining them to all parties involved will set the right expectations for corporate efforts and also establish a benchmark for measurement.

Other Ways to Give Back through Your Profession

You might find that giving back via your chosen profession appeals to you on many levels. It could ramp up your passion for your profession, help you meet like-minded people, see the real grassroots impact of your work, and help you reach a piece of the world you've always been drawn to, either by traveling or helping from home.

Here are a couple of other ways you can engage in professional humanitarian organizations, including a few more "Without Borders" organizations:

Lawyers Without Borders: The Lawyers Without Borders (LWOB) pool of international attorneys offers pro bono legal services to underprivileged societies. LWOB was conceived on a frigid Super Bowl Sunday in 2000. Approaching fifty, Connecticut attorney Christina Storm dreamt of more humanitarian adventures. She remembered how much she loved traveling the world as a young woman and how she once longed to work for the United Nations. On a whim, she searched the Internet for "Lawyers Without Borders." She asked her husband Jim if she could borrow his credit card. He said, "Chris, this is a really important game. Here's the card, but can you do me a favor and not interrupt again until it's over?"

In four feverish hours, Storm secured a domain, created her site, and emailed colleagues. Now when Storm interrupts her husband during a hot game? "He stops everything dead in its tracks and gives me his undivided attention," she says. "We laugh often about that moment."

LWOB provides the legal punch found in the most prestigious firms, Storm says. "We combine the resources of junior associates, who do the research, with the guidance and wisdom of senior lawyers. This allows students to work on real cases of international consequence." One current LWOB project: shoring up the inheritance laws for the twelve million African children orphaned by AIDS. www. lawyerswithoutborders.org

"I could wait twenty years and build a memorial to those who died of AIDS. Or I can do something now."

—*Cameron Sinclair,*
Architecture for Humanity founder

Teachers Without Borders: Also mentioned on page 73, Teachers Without Borders is launching a new e-learning system so the world's fifty-nine million teachers can share curriculum and teaching methods, says TWB director Fred Mednick. For instance, Raphael Oko, a Nigerian educator, tapped TWB for the best HIV/AIDS education material and trained thousands of teachers. His efforts have boosted school attendance 23 percent and voluntary HIV/AIDS testing 18 percent. Teachers in the United States have also sent supplies and teaching materials for Oko's refugee-camp school, which serves nine hundred students. Mednick says he feels privileged to do what he does. "When you shake someone's hand, that's the time you truly feel your own," he says. "Well, I get to shake all these different hands, learn about who I am, and what I was put on the planet for." www.teacherswithoutborders.org

🐾 **Engineers Without Borders–USA:** EWB–USA teams student engineers with seasoned engineers, plus other professionals such as architects, anthropologists, and business people. Volunteers work to deliver clean water, sanitation and irrigation systems, and renewable energy to developing countries.

EWB–USA has been called the Blueprint Brigade by *Time* magazine because of how its members wade into jagged Thai ravines, Mayan communities, and villages in forty-five other countries to help install systems for clean water, alternative energy, irrigation, and sanitation for people in the developing world. EWB–USA, which has helped revive the heart and soul of engineering, works to create a safer, more stable world by addressing the roots of conflict—poverty and lack of access to basic human need, from safe drinking water to power to education. EWB–USA was founded by Bernard Amadei, a civil engineering professor at the University of Colorado, after he had a seemingly random conversation with a native of Belize who was landscaping his yard. The landscaper asked Amadei if he'd be willing to help his Mayan village with its water distribution problems.

A few years later, Amadei went to visit Belize and saw little girls carrying water back and forth to their villages, which made them miss out on school. He returned to Boulder, Colorado, recruited engineering students and a local civil engineering expert, and they designed a water distribution system. When Amadei returned to Belize with ten students, they installed the low-cost system, which features a pump fueled by a local waterfall. It now provides a steady flow of water to the community, which helped support it, and the little girls Amadei met were finally able to go to school.

After his experience in Belize, Amadei found himself mulling a lifelong dream—to use his engineering skills to solve problems in the developing world.

"Improving the lives of billions of people whose main concern is to stay alive by the end of each day on our planet is no longer an option for engineers. It's an obligation," he says.

Engineers, students and seasoned, agree. When Amadei founded EWB–USA in 2001, it had eighteen members. Now it has more than twelve thousand members and more than three hundred projects in forty-five countries. EWB–USA's volunteers have installed wind-powered turbines in Guatemala, solar panels for emergency lighting at a hospital in Rwanda, and computers in a remote village in Nepal.

It's also speaking to students across the country, and at least 180 student chapters have formed. Allison Poulignot is active in the University of Missouri–Rolla chapter: "I'd never been out of the country before, but all I knew was I wanted to help." Poulignot taught impoverished Bolivians to build latrines and showers and access clean drinking water. "Ask anyone there what their most pressing need is, and they will tell you, 'Aqua es vida.' Water is life," she says.

Sixty-six-year-old Steve Forbes is one EWB–USA member who's traveled extensively to support communities in the developing world. He worked with student engineers to help build a reservoir that will bring irrigation water to more than ten thousand Cambodian villagers suffering from severe food shortages since heavy rains destroyed their levee in 2000. Without a water storage system for rice and other crops, villagers are often forced to go into mosquito-laden jungles to harvest wood to sell. Sadly, the jungles hide deadly land mines left from the Khmer Rouge and government conflicts that raged until 1998.

Though busy managing his Texas firm, Forbes can't look away from extreme poverty. He's also teamed with students on safe drinking water projects and other enterprises in Ghana, Thailand, and Uganda. "My personal goals are to contribute to the eradication of poverty, which leads to disease, war and inadequate resources," says Forbes.

The Engineers Without Borders chapter at Montana State University (MSU) works with villagers in the western Kenya region of Khwisero to install small water wells with a huge impact.

Forty engineering and other student volunteers have installed five water wells so that three thousand people can enjoy clean drinking water. The flowing water also liberates the young girls to carry school books and finally get an education—instead of walking miles each day to fetch contaminated water from streams.

Working on vacations and summer breaks, the Montana State students have formed relationships with and worked alongside Kenyans like twenty-three-year-old Nina Omwereme Oyamo, a teacher's aid. Oyamo worked to help her school get its first well for clean drinking water. "I have discovered that you Americans are friendly people and that you work without borders. Water in this village of ours is the most important priority," Oyamo says.

Less than 40 percent of Kenyans have access to clean drinking water. To plan and dig wells, the Montana State students have mobilized and worked with elders, parents suffering from AIDS, and children hungry to attend school. "We work alongside and involve the local people to take leadership and ownership of the water projects so they can realize a sustainable and healthy source of water," says Katy Hansen, a chapter member.

The EWB–USA chapter has made a ten-year commitment to install water wells at fifty-eight western Kenyan schools.

MSU mechanical engineering junior Griffin Stevens also found that one of the most rewarding aspects was seeing what a difference he was making in the lives of others—and getting to know members of the community. Stevens stayed with the family of Francis Ashira, one of the two men who initiated the water project. In addition to caring for his own family and grandfather, Ashira had taken in his brother's children when his life was taken by AIDS. Despite this already strained situation, "they put us up, and were just the nicest people," Stevens said. "The children were so happy to get a well, and the community members were so supportive and thankful. It was quite an amazing experience."

As a final people-to-people connection between Africans and Americans, the EWB–MSU team also initiated a pen-pal program between students in Kenya and students in Bozeman, Montana. This year, the team collected over 140 letters from seventh graders at the three schools where the wells were drilled. EWB members brought them back to the United States and distributed them to seventh graders in several schools in Bozeman.

You can support EWB–USA in a variety of capacities, from donating support for its ongoing projects to joining or forming a chapter. www.ewb-usa.org

◦ **Doctors Without Borders:** Maybe the most well known of all the "Without Borders" groups, Doctors Without Borders was founded in 1971 as a nonprofit, nongovernmental international medical humanitarian organization. The primary focus of this organization is to provide emergency medical aid to people in sixty countries affected by armed conflict, epidemics, natural or man-made disasters, or exclusion from health care.

Doctors Without Borders hires medical, administrative, and logistical support personnel to help provide medical care to people in need across the globe. Other opportunities include volunteering in the organization's New York office as well as unpaid internships. www.doctorswithoutborders.org

◦ **MBAs Without Borders:** MBAs Without Borders was founded in Canada in 2004 and recently opened MWB–USA, with an office in San Francisco, in 2007. The goal of this organization is to match experienced business and entrepreneurial volunteers with local businesses and NGOs in developing countries. The basic idea behind the work of MWB is that business can and must play a crucial role in alleviating poverty in developing countries and that the valuable skills of MBAs are greatly needed in the developing world. MWB partners with projects throughout Africa, Asia, and Latin America, providing a wide range of business support, including training for management and staff in finance, accounting, strategy, marketing, human resources, business development, and much more.

The typical volunteer is on average thirty-two years old, speaks multiple languages, and has extensive experience in business. An understanding of the needs of businesses and organizations in developing countries is also important.

For those who are unable to travel to overseas projects but would still like to use their expertise to aid in the efforts of MWB, there are opportunities to volunteer from home as well. www.mbaswithoutborders.org

Software Without Borders: Software Without Borders is a nonprofit foundation that develops custom software for underfunded businesses and organizations in both developed and developing countries. The premise behind the operations of this organization is that the success of information technology in the developed world cannot be replicated in the developing world by simply putting desktop computers in schools, governments, or the hands of private businesses. Rather, there is a need in developing countries for complex software packages that allow businesses to reduce their inventories, farmers to better plan their crops, governments to better collect taxes, and so on.

Any organization that has a need for custom software can review the project requirements on the Software Without Borders website to see if their project qualifies for development. The organization must then submit a request form via the website. Decisions about whether to undertake a project are based on need and available resources. www.softwarewithoutborders.com

&o **Amazon Promise:** For fourteen years, Amazon Promise volunteers have worked alongside local physicians to provide health care to people living in the upper Amazon Basin of Peru. That includes thirty-two jungle villages as well as two poor districts in the city of Iquis. Physicians of all specialties are welcome. www.amazonpromise.org

&o **Health Volunteers Overseas:** HVO sends health-care professionals to train local personnel in Africa, Asia, Latin America, and the Caribbean. Specialists in internal medicine, pediatrics, dermatology, burn management, wound care, hematology, and anesthesia, as well as surgeons (hand, orthopedic, oral, and maxillofacial), are sent on assignments of two to four weeks. www. hvousa.org

&o **Medical Teams International:** Short-term assignments of one to four weeks are available in Africa, Asia, Latin America, and Europe. Health-care professionals in anesthesia, cardiology, community health, emergency services, endoscopy, ENT, family practice, general surgery, HIV/AIDS, ICU/CCU, infectious diseases, internal medicine, midwifery, neurology, ob-gyn, pediatrics, urology, and other areas are welcome. www.medicalteams.org

🐾 **Veterinarians Without Borders:** Founded in 2004, Veterinarians Without Borders is a Canada-based nonprofit organization whose mission is to work with those in need to foster the health of animals, people, and the environments that sustain them. Individuals with animal-health skills are welcome to become members, whether they're veterinarians or not. The organization works around the globe with projects related to the health of aquaculture and land-based farm animals, urban domestic animals, and wildlife, as well as public and ecosystem health.

With the understanding that livestock and wildlife play a vital role in the health and well-being of communities in many parts of the world, VWB/VSF works to provide clinical, educational, and investigative services, program evaluation and development, and emergency response and relief throughout the world. www.vwb-vsf.ca

Helping in the United States: Concerned Corporate Citizens on the Move

Look at Home Depot, where every store has a Team Depot captain to spearhead employee volunteering in the community. Take Hewlett-Packard, Aetna, or Cargill. Companies are totally amping up their employee volunteering efforts in their respective communities. They know that doing good in their own backyards is not only the right thing to do, but it also fosters a happier, more committed work force. Plus, community service gives employees hands-on engagement with environmental, social, educational, and other challenges. Volunteers see themselves as part of the solution—which, in return, sharpens their on-the-job performance and motivation. Volunteering gives employees greater meaning, both inside and outside the company.

If you want to join the sea change and harness the power of your employees for good, there's no need to reinvent the proverbial wheel. Go online and check out what other companies are doing, from small shops to mega-corporations. Network with other companies around you. Find out how they launched their efforts and how they're managed. Aetna, for instance, offers community volunteering in its professional development program. At Aetna, service work is considered a great way to develop employee skills and support professional growth.

Some firms promote regular Habitat for Humanity builds or low-income house painting during the annual Day of Caring. Others spring to action with disaster relief, which is always needed. After the catastrophic flooding in Cedar Rapids, Iowa, in 2007, John Deere dove in and funded flood relief, which also motivated many to get out and help clean up entire blocks in downtown Cedar Rapids wiped out by flooding.

Cargill created a unique program, Water Matters, which encourages employees, retirees, and their families to learn about local water-quality issues and to get directly involved in programs and activities that address those issues in their own homes, offices, and communities. As part of Water Matters,

Cargill given hundreds of its employees time off to volunteer for the nonprofit organization Living Land and Waters, an environmental organization that promotes river stewardship and protects natural resources.

Cargill employees have donated their time to Living Lands and Waters river cleanups on the Illinois, Ohio, Missouri, Mississippi, and Potomac rivers. Cargill also supports the organization's river-education seminars and river-bottom restoration projects.

Living Lands and Waters could easily be a rewarding volunteer match for your company. It was created in 1998 after then-twenty-two-year old Chad Pregracke got sick of seeing all the garbage that littered the Mississippi River—the nation's greatest river and the river on which he grew up. Growing restless after state and federal agencies tuned out his plea to save the river, he decided that if no one else would clean it up, he would. "With no model to go by, but armed with bottomless passion, extreme persistence, and infectious energy, Chad Pregracke's mission has evolved into the only 'industrial strength' river cleanup operation in the world," says Tammy Becker, Living Lands and Waters education coordinator.

Chad and his eight barge–dwelling, jon boat–yielding, garbage-busting crews and over forty thousand volunteers have removed approximately five million pounds of refuse from some of America's most historic rivers. Chad's vision has attracted an abundance of national media attention, accolades, awards, and corporate support.

In 2003, Living Lands and Waters broadened its scope to educate teachers, students, and citizens on the importance and value of river ecosystems and the need for keeping them clean. "Since then, over 1,700 people have participated in workshops aboard our floating classroom. Also in 2003, Living Lands and Waters started a river-bottom restoration 'branch' of our organization and has planted 30,000 native hardwood trees in the floodplain. We recently started a nursery for our MillionTrees Project, in which we are aiming to grow and plant at least one million trees within the next five to ten years," Becker says. "Our reach continues to expand as we are currently making plans for a massive restoration project on the Upper Mississippi River as well as a new floating classroom, aiming specifically at young kids."

Many corporations like to develop team-based volunteering efforts to boost the fun potential. Some Colorado engineering firms bring out their inner sand sculptor and play on the beach for a good cause each year. To raise money for the Denver chapter of Engineering Without Borders–USA, the nonprofit for which I work, employees pull out all the stops—and sand shovels, buckets, and water spritzers—to design prize-winning sand sculptures. In 2008 sculptures ranged from the Great Wall of China and the Olympic rings to a sleeping dragon and an African village with children.

If your corporation wants to launch its own community volunteering effort, still another great touchstone is Points of Light Foundation. On the site are great tools, resources, and examples of corporate service programs and why they are growing. For more information, check out www.pointsoflight.org. Again, you can also look on www.idealist.org and see what volunteer programs exist in your community and to join forces with some existing service programs.

Finally, if you're a manager, know that your employees will likely rally around you, no matter what direction your service goes in. People are more than willing to help; they just need someone to step up and give them a compelling reason to. If you want to start a new company volunteer program, here are seven tips.

- Offer your employees paid time off to volunteer. Hewlett-Packard, for instance, gives its employees up to four hours per month to volunteer in their communities, whether they're tutoring math students in area schools or building a Habitat for Humanity home.
- Designate an employee volunteer or service coordinator to spearhead give-back efforts in your community
- Treat the volunteering program as professionally as any other. Hold regular meetings, set goals, be accountable, and show results.
- Let the fun begin. Provide food, hats, t-shirts, or breakfast at your company's service events. Let the media know so employees can enjoy the limelight as they do good work.
- Team up. Partner with other companies and nonprofits doing great work.
- Tell the story. If you're choosing a nonprofit or cause to support, make sure you tell its story in a way that inspires and motivates people to give back.
- Be the change you want to see. Lead by example and volunteer yourself so you inspire those around you to join in.

One Volunteer's Journey

My sister, Joan Conrad, is Deere & Company's world-wide supply management manager of communications and training. Here is her story of how Deere & Company developed part of its give-back program around the country. It shows how great ideas can eventually take on even greater meaning and go on to ripple out across the company.

"In the late summer of 2001, our corporate supply management group at Deere & Company in Moline, Illinois, was searching for a different way to roll out its strategic plan for the next fiscal year. Several of our people convinced our vice-president (it wasn't too hard) to allow our employees to take part in a half-day volunteer event that we called the Day of Caring. We worked with the United Way to identify projects throughout the community that employees could take on in teams. Employees from different departments would work together. We felt the event would develop camaraderie, allow employees to network, improve our community, and create enthusiasm and pride among our people. We set the date for the event: September 12. Little did we know how meaningful the Day of Caring would be.

"When the events of September 11, 2001, unfolded, some questioned whether the Day of Caring should go on. Employees responded with an overwhelming "Yes!" The next day, they expressed their grief through their hearts and hands-on projects throughout the Quad Cities. More than 150 employees weeded, scraped, painted, cleaned, planted, visited seniors, swept, hammered, nailed, sawed, sanded, and scrubbed. At the end of the day, grateful United Way agencies expressed their thanks.

"Inspired by the work of the John Deere employees, the Day of Caring has become a day-long community-wide event that brings together volunteers from many employers and other organizations throughout the Quad Cities. More than one thousand people volunteer for the event, which serves as the official kickoff for the Quad City United Way campaign. And we've been told by the United Way that our event has been the inspiration for similar Day of Caring events around the company.

"This year, I was the co-leader for a team that worked at the local YWCA. Ten of my team members primed and painted four rooms and a hallway; two replaced screens, hung curtain rods, and did carpentry odd jobs; and ten of us sewed eighty-four yards of fabric into curtains for day-care rooms, so the rooms could be darkened when the children take naps."

PART THREE

Into The World—And Back Home Again

So by now, you're ready to rock. You're eager to dive in and flex your change-agent muscles, whether you go abroad or stay at home. This last section gives you one final springboard from which to launch your give-back journey—and help make it as incredible as possible. It also helps you return home in the best possible light, savoring what you've experienced, and empowered to continue making change happen.

As you gear up to head out, take to heart the sage advice on the following page from Joshua Machinga, who sees volunteers come through his African village each year. It's really fantastic guidance, whether you go far afield or serve right where you are.

"Come with an open mind, ready to absorb a flood of new information and a new frame of reference. Leave your expectations at home. Observe without judgment until you fully understand all the factors. If something strikes you as being '"backward,'" objectively consider why it is acceptable in this culture. You will probably find valid reasons. I do recommend that during your first few weeks or months, simply observe, learn, and try to understand the culture. See how things 'work' here. Try to remember that there is never just one right way to do something. You most likely will see many things that are 'backward,' but are common and appropriate here. Just remember that often there is no right or wrong."

—*Joshua Machinga,*
a village program director for Village Volunteers,
Common Ground, in Kiminini, Kenya

CHAPTER TEN

Ensuring a Safe, Successful Trip

For those of you who have chosen to go abroad to give back, once you've chosen your organization and your volunteer opportunity, done your homework, and started packing—or maybe already got a bag at the door—make sure you've taken care of the essentials: your volunteer organization will have shared with you its more in-depth list of pre-trip recommendations, tailored to your destination. Make sure you've heeded all the suggestions. So with that in mind, this is just a quick refresher, a basic "do-good checklist" to make sure you're set and ready to have a successful experience.

Your Do-Good Checklist

❑ **Proper clothing:** As you know, many countries are much more modest in their dress, especially for women. Respect their customs and follow the clothing guidelines from your volunteer and travel organization. You also want to make sure you're protecting your skin with the right clothing, whether you'll be working in the blistering sun all day or wading into swamps.

❑ **Meds and over-the-counter treatments:** Make sure you have enough of your own prescriptions, sunscreens, and malaria meds, if recommended by your physician or local government health officials. Your physician may also recommend you take a whole host of over-the-counter treatments for everything from nausea to common colds. Don't forget your insect repellant if you're heading to a tropical zone. Again, check with your volunteer organization and physician for their recommendations. Simple things like tampons, aspirin, or cough medicine may not be available where you're headed, so pack what you might need.

❑ **Background on your destination:** Learn as much as you can about the region to which you're headed. The more you know, the richer the experience. Make sure you learn a bit of the language, too.

❑ **Money/communications:** Again, this will all be in your pre-departure recommendations from your volunteer organization, but make sure you're covered for currency, credit cards, and phone cards. As far as cash goes, organizations often recommend that you wait and exchange what you think you'll need after you arrive and check out the local exchange rates.

❑ **Immunizations:** While it's not critical if you forget your phone card, you don't want to fudge on these. Make sure you're covered. Check with your local government health officials and personal physician, and also check with the U.S. Centers for Disease Control's website (www.cdc.gov)

to see what is recommended for immunizations, by region, since conditions on the ground can change.

❑ **Travel documents:** Double-check you've got your passport, visa, if necessary, and proof of international health insurance.

❑ **Miscellaneous:** What do you need to make this a comfortable, successful trip? Cameras, ear plugs, a journal, a pair of comfortable socks after a long day, a few snapshots from home, a relaxing paperback? Keep your valuables at home. You won't need them, and it will be safer.

And Don't Forget to Pack the Right Perspective

This trip will show you what you're made of, at the core. It will also help you get some valuable perspective on your own world and what really matters. To maximize the experience and savor it to the hilt, make sure you also bring along the best of yourself to your destination. Here are five key things you don't want to leave home without.

1. **Respect:** We all have our own horror stories. There's nothing worse than being around obnoxious, disrespectful travelers. Don't be one of them. Be mindful that you're a guest in the countries you're visiting. People you meet may be living in mud huts and cooking over open fires, but they live with dignity and courage and deserve your respect. Don't be the paternalistic, overbearing, smarter-than-you volunteer marching in to fix their world. If you criticize their ways and practices, you can't begin to understand

them. Immerse yourself in their culture, learn about their values, hopes, and plans—and work at building the relationship they'd love to have with you.

2. **Acceptance:** Life is very different in the developing world. Along with respect, bring a healthy measure of acceptance. Try to accept that projects run more slowly and often unpredictably. Electricity often goes out; meetings may start way late; people walk for miles because they don't own even a bicycle; and amazingly, they often take more time to talk and laugh and enjoy one another. (More about this in the final chapter on what *we* can glean from other cultures!)

Be more realistic about what you can actually accomplish during your stay. Whether you're helping improve water and sanitation systems or building a nursery school, everything may be more complex and move at a different pace than you expected. If you're used to being in control—amped on accomplishments and powering through your day—step back a bit. Breathe, slow down, and try to appreciate how good it feels to connect on a more human level without the tyranny of a "to-do" list that has to get done. Keep adjusting your expectations every few hours. Your experience is as much about making new friends around the world as completing anything, though you will undoubtedly be rolling up your sleeves a lot.

Check your assumptions that you'll come in and save the day—or even completely finish a project. Maybe you'll get the walls of a school painted but not touch the books or desks. Maybe you'll count the number of migratory birds in the Amazon, not knowing if your efforts will boost their survival rate in the near term. Surrender to the idea that you're one of a rising tide of volunteers, and if each of us does a little, great things can happen, together, over time.

"Volunteers can't think they can change the world in one week, but they should know that their presence and desire to help has such a great impact on the entire world. Each small effort changes so much. I tend of think of our volunteers as 'ambassadors for change.'"

—*Catherine McMillan,*
Globe Aware

3. **Openness:** Have an open heart and mind, Globe Aware's Catherine McMillan advises. "To open up to understanding cultural differences, you need to let go of being judgmental." So try to spend more time listening to local people to understand their perspective. Try to look more from your heart, not your mind. See how precious people and landscapes really are. Try to sense just how connected we are, and notice how similar our dreams, hopes, suffering, and worlds are. Slow down and be present to the amazing people you'll have the privilege of working alongside or staying with. Let them change *your* world.

4. **Patience:** Always challenging for us full-tilt Westerners, patience is perfected in the developing world. I learned much about it from Alice, a former Ugandan refugee who now

works at BeadforLife's Kampala office. One day we were in the tiny office hallway, big enough for just a few people, making a copy on the one small, slow copy machine. Tired of waiting, I was frustrated and trying to wrench my single copy from the machine before it was ready. Alice started laughing. "Wait for it. Wait for it," she said softly, teasing me. And when the copy came, she slowly smiled and presented it to me as if it were a shining gift. Which it was. We twitchy, impatient, rushed Americans. Being patient, appreciating the small things—who couldn't stand a bit more of that?

5. **Flexibility:** The ability to be highly flexible and adapt to unforeseen situations is also key. I read a story about a volunteer who showed up at his village in India expecting to do great, virtuous things, educate the people, and save the children—right away, or at least in the first forty-eight hours. But first it turned out he had to help chase wild animals from the village's chicken coop, because if the chickens were lost, well then, it would be devastating to

"At any moment, the best-laid plan may have to be put aside because of a death in the community, inclement weather, lack of funding, or a multitude of other factors. Life in a rural setting is unpredictable, particularly for those who are just visiting. If you tend to need to feel in control, try to leave those feelings at home. The benefits to you will be a greater peace of mind and appreciation for the intangible contributions you are making to the community."

—*Shana Green,*
Village Volunteers founder

the village. Then, it started pouring, since it was the monsoon season, so that meant transporting the chickens to higher ground so they'd be safe. And so went much of his first day. Not saving people, directly, but saving chickens, which actually were lifesavers for the people.

If you're used to being at the top of your game in your profession, this much flexibility can be challenging for the über-professional in you.

"You can be the best English teacher or doctor or engineer, but if you don't have the right expectation and ability to be flexible, those skills don't matter," Cross-Cultural Solution's executive director Steven Rosenthal says.

So be kind to yourself, and practice being a bit more flexible in every moment. This is a world where you don't always have to be a human "doer" and worship at the altar of machinelike productivity. Stay on an even keel; work to strengthen the relationships you're building; and enjoy the sense of community around you. If you fume about the weather, the lack of routine, the work delays, the unforeseen, you'll miss the amazing liveliness all around you. Author Alan Cohen says when you're feeling frustrated, back off; when you're feeling centered again, then act. Through it all, appreciate what's positive, stay open, and then see what happens.

One Volunteer's Journey: How One Man Returned Home and Reinvented His Life

Dan Polk, a California teacher and former Amigos de las Américas volunteer, is exactly the kind of volunteer that the Building Bridges Coalition envisions when it plans for one hundred thousand volunteers by 2010. Polk came home from volunteering overseas engaged, mobilized, and awake. And then he turned around and remade his world. Along with friends Jason and Jenni Doherty, he's founding a new school in Kenya for students from as many tribes as possible to "create a new generation of Kenyans that can look past the heated tribal issues of the not-so-distant past."

The new Kenyan school is named the Daraja Academy, which means "bridge" in Swahili. Polk and the Dohertys plan to open their first class of twenty-five female students in early 2009. "Africa has long been exploited and neglected," says Polk. "I believe in the students that I met here. When I visit their classrooms, their drive and determination are palpable. The resources and country infrastructure are not. For me, in some ways, it is simple. I have seen poverty and a lack of resources for the young in Kenya. I know people with resources, who are far from poverty. We put the two together, and that's the bridge that is Daraja."

Polk's busy spreading the word, building a community of kindred supporters around the country, and raising funds: $27 funds a fully loaded backpack; $21 funds towels, shampoo, and soap to keep a student squeaky clean for a year; $3,579 funds a student for one year, including transportation, room and board, books and extras, and so on.

"I've always been a creator of community, but this has made me a global community creator. I am now connected to hundreds of people all over the world who are in some way connected to Africa," he says. "Connecting to these various people inspires me every day. Working for Daraja puts me in regular contact with truly good and devoted people, who continually are looking outside themselves for fulfillment—not in material possessions, but in making the world a place of balance, where chronic hunger, poverty, disease, and destitution are not tolerated as an accepted norm." And in the process of fund-raising, speaking, sharing, and asking for support, Polk says he's found his voice even more: "I have always had some level of confidence in public speaking. But when I speak now, it isn't always just with my voice. I feel myself speaking with the voice of hundreds of students whose names I don't yet know but who are silently asking me to continue to learn, grow, and have hope for their futures."

CHAPTER ELEVEN

Coming Home

Engaging More

"I used to say I'll get culture shock when I go back home."

—*Paul Theroux*

If you choose to volunteer abroad, coming home can really feel like a reverse tsunami of emotions and physical sensations. "The cultural shock coming back was harder to deal with than going there," recalls Amanda Anderson-Green about returning from her time in Ghana.

Granted, you might be exhilarated to be on U.S. soil again, with coffee shops, steaming-hot showers, twenty-four-hour convenience stores, and your own bed at the ready. But the gaping contrast between this world and the world you've returned from can feel very jarring and unsettling. You might find yourself longing to be back at your project, missing the tight sense of community and camaraderie you enjoyed.

My son and I found trekking through the Thai countryside, volunteering, and enjoying ourselves with the other volunteers so much fun, we felt let down when we returned home. Even though it was the height of the holiday season, we still missed our group and remarked about how isolated we Americans, with our nuclear families, can be.

You might find yourself sorely missing the incredible people you met, especially if they were your host family or treated you like family, as Anderson-Green found: "The Ghanaian culture was so warm and inviting, and I was really drawn to it. It felt really closed off when I came home. I saw people just walking around, not talking to one another. Everyone was very business-like, hyper-efficient."

It's natural to feel a little disoriented, vulnerable, even raw, when you return. And you're bound to miss the people you met, both the local people and the other volunteers. That kind of intimate, more meaningful connection is one of the true gifts of volunteering abroad—but one of the hardest things to leave behind, especially overnight.

Kimberly Walker, who volunteered for four months in Tanzania with Global Service Corps, said that returning home was probably the most difficult part of her entire journey. "I knew that I would come home and things would be the same as when I left. Four months isn't very long, and yet I felt so different. I was sad to think that I would no longer wake up every morning and experience something new and exhilarating. I was afraid that the happiness I knew in Africa wouldn't return home with me. I feared that I would forget about everything that I had learned while on my journey. And that my life would just continue on as it was before."

Hopefully, these suggestions and thoughts can help ease your re-entry and help you retain some of the best of your experience:

1. First, sleep, rest, make sure your physical health is sound. If you're feeling any physical discomforts, from fevers to chills or diarrhea, check in with your doctor to make sure you didn't bring any unwanted microbial stowaways home with you.

2. Then, take some time to reflect. Look at your images, journal recording, souvenirs and think about the people you met, the experiences you had, the gains or setbacks you experienced. Scroll back to some of the best stories, moments-in-time, rewards, celebrations. Begin to let the scope of all you've experienced begin to settle around you.

3. Get some perspective. Ask yourself some questions to better understand what happened and how it affected you. What were the highlights? What were the low points? If you could tell your best friend or partner about the absolute best moment there—and the most challenging one—what would you share? What did you learn about the country you traveled to? What did you learn about yourself in the frustrating moments? What did you learn about the people? How are they different from the people here?

4. Ask yourself what you came to understand about our own country. What do we do well—and what can we do differently? How were we viewed by the villagers and others

you met? How do our values differ from the country in which you were immersed? How might you be part of the ongoing transformation into a more globally connected— and harmonious—world?

5. Get in touch with your overall feelings about this experience. Accept that you might feel alternately raw and elated, galvanized to do more and overwhelmed at the immensity of what's required. You might be thrilled to rediscover your favorite foods and creature comforts again—but sober, knowing that your new friends overseas might be going to bed tonight in a mud hut on an empty stomach. Accept that you have a more awakened consciousness. You can't look away anymore, you may discover, from the world's suffering. It may lead you to rethink and reexamine your life now. It may prompt you to rework your world a bit—or a lot. But accept that you might feel a little confused and unsure as you come to grips with it all. And that's okay, too.

6. Be grateful: Be grateful that you had this amazing experience. Be grateful that you had the amazing opportunity to care about others outside of your experience. Be grateful that you were daring, curious, open. Be grateful that you did it! Appreciate yourself, and be open to what can come next. Be grateful that though so much remains to be done in the developing world, so much is happening.

7. Let the experience change you. Don't resist what you may be feeling or sensing. Maybe some pieces of your life do

need to change. Maybe seeing how much more slowly the rest of the world moves can help you slow down a bit more in your own. Maybe it's time to rethink some values and choices. Let your volunteering influence your days and routines, even a little. Let the memories, stories, and experiences permeate your choices, from your conversations to your relationships to your local citizenship to your consumer purchases.

8. Stay in touch with some of the people you met, if that feels right. Having enjoyed such a keener sense of community, try to stay connected to some of the volunteers you met and maybe some of the local people you met at the projects where you volunteered. Some volunteer-vacation organizations have created alumni gatherings you can attend.

9. Do a kind of personal inventory: Who are you now? How have you changed, and what do you know about yourself? How have your values shifted? What strengths did you discover about yourself? Do you want to volunteer again or engage from home?

10. Be open to learning more about the world you visited. I found myself pulling out maps and books, getting insights from others, and researching more on the Internet: Who were those tribes, those refugees? What have they experienced? Why is it so hard to get a school started in the developing world? What is happening to help the AIDS orphans? Once you open up that window to the world, you realize there's so much we don't understand—but can

learn. Part of the pleasure of coming home is extending your trip, in a way, by studying and reading more about what you've experienced.

11. Be understanding and patient with people at home. Accept that you may feel profoundly changed, but the people here may still see you as the same. They may even want you to stay the same, since they liked and enjoyed who you were before. Plus, they may not share your passion for the world you've fallen in love with. Be patient and do what you can to find kindred people.

12. Build your kindred community here. Attend international festivals at your local university; network with other volunteers. Go to lectures and book signings on global issues. Connect with others online, and blog about your stories and experiences.

13. Decide what happens next: Can you inspire others to reach out to the developing world in their own way? Are you drawn at all to sharing your story to a wider audience, maybe through presentations, YouTube postings, newspaper guest opinions, or school appearances? Want to organize an event to raise awareness? How can you continue to "be the change"? Amanda Anderson-Green's volunteer vacation sharpened her hunger to continue studying infectious diseases and amp up her health-care advocacy. "I am listening to that instinct in me that says, 'It's just not right that so much of the world doesn't even have basic health care,'" she says.

When you're volunteering abroad, there are so many new experiences to take in and process. It's often not until you return home that you really have a chance to sit, reflect, and find some meaning in what you experienced. Try to pause and take full advantage of that space between your two worlds to look at what you've just been through, as this volunteer did.

One Volunteer's Journey: "My First Emotion Was the Desire to Go Straight Back 'Home' to Peru"

"Coming home from Peru and reentering my daily life in San Francisco was a challenging adjustment period. The moment I walked back into my flat, I barely recognized my own life. I had changed, and everything now seems so foreign. My first emotion was the desire to go straight back 'home' to Peru. I desperately missed the kids and the other volunteers. But then I realized that what I had learned and how I had lived in Peru was something I needed to incorporate into my own daily practice. In Peru, my routine consisted of comforting, as well as laughing with, children who have nothing. My priorities shifted greatly, which allowed me to see that my life was bigger and wasn't meant just for me. All of my personal 'challenges' that I'd temporarily left behind still existed, but my experience allowed me to approach the roadblocks with compassion, gratitude, and loving-kindness. I am still and will forever be a work in progress.

But I thank God every day for the seven weeks in Peru

that have changed me inside. At one time or another we all ask ourselves what our purpose is. When you hit that point, I encourage you to go outside of yourself and give. You don't have to leave the country, but perhaps it's a simple act of kindness during your day. You will see your own value and that each of us has a part to play in changing this world. That gives each of us a purpose and importance." —Robyn Liston, a marketing manager in San Francisco who spent seven weeks on a Globe Aware trip.

Conclusion

Let the Developing World Change Ours

"Hope is back on me!" Alice seems to almost sing those words, her voice somehow carrying no sense of the horror she's endured. Alice's journey has been anything but hopeful. She is a Ugandan refugee—one of more than 1.5 million people displaced from their homes over the last eighteen years by brutal civil war in northern Uganda. Alice's parents died when she was very young; her stepmother abused her; and rebels burst into her home one day and killed her husband. Her little boy, Valentino, was born on Valentine's Day; his life was supposed to be more loving. But soon after his father died, Alice discovered she was HIV-positive—and so was her son. "But now I know love can cure anything," Alice says. "Hope is back on me!"

I met Alice during my time in Uganda with BeadforLife and was drawn to her because she had a wisdom of the heart I wanted to learn more about. As I discovered in Uganda and later on my volunteer vacation in Thailand, we have so much to receive from the gorgeous human beings we meet in our travels, many of whom were forced to cross borders and cultures with nothing. Nothing but blinding humanity. That this humanity remains not just intact but a North Star for us is staggering.

Most of the people you'll have the pleasure of meeting aren't waving their fists in the air, threatening to take anyone down, even though they've often suffered many injustices and cruelties. They aren't bitter or vengeful, even though their bodies often bear the scars of weapons, diseases, poverty, and domestic abuse.

Instead, they have a grace that we can learn from—are hungry to learn from, I think. With dignity, they "brush the dust off their souls," as one Ugandan woman told me. And working alongside them, we learn how to do so as well.

How can we trust, as they do, in the generosity and grace of complete strangers? How can we regain our humanity in a world that often seems to have come unhinged?

How can we heal from slights and pain and not inflict torture in return? How can we stop fighting? How do we transform suffering into soul force and dance and celebrate and laugh, not knowing what tomorrow may bring? The truth is that people living in the developing world have many gifts to give us as well.

They can help us rediscover what a miracle it is to be that awake: we, too, can celebrate the air we breathe, the clothes we wear, the meals we eat, and the roofs over our heads. We complain if we have too much house to maintain; they are beyond grateful for a small dwelling. I want to learn more about being that love-struck with life—and living more peacefully.

I wear my favorite BeadforLife green bracelet as a touchstone to remind me of five lessons I learned from the incredible women of Uganda.

1. **Connect:** We are here for one another. We are here to enjoy, serve, and love one another. When we connect with what we have in common—while putting up medical clinics in war-torn villages or listening to one another's stories over fires late at night on the shores of distant oceans—we feel our inherent oneness. We draw our mutual worlds closer. And the more we connect, the more we appreciate one another, the more it becomes unthinkable that we would ever war or tear one another down.

2. **Neither my past nor my future defines who I really am:** The women I met refuse to let their experiences, no matter how horrific, block their joy. And they forgive those who hurt them. As Alice says, "Even if you hurt me, I won't put you in my mind. That's it! If someone hurts you, you forgive and don't do bad things back."

3. **Be present:** Slow down; stop rushing through life. Enjoy the process, not knowing where the journey ends. Savor the little things, express your joy, share your sorrow. Be awake to life now.

4. **Transform struggle into triumph:** The beaders of Beadfor-Life even wrote a song, "We Dance When We Are Struggling," to show that we can always choose to transcend suffering and turn it into something greater.

5. **Most of all, be continuously grateful:** Gratitude can flow as naturally as sunshine bathes the mango blossoms in their world, or the blades of grass in ours. The people I met from the developing world, from the former Lost Boys of Sudan to the Thai refugees, are acutely mindful

of good health, hot food, basic transportation, affordable medicine, and life in general. I want to be that grateful. Grateful for my own world and grateful that we're discovering one another around the world as never before.

The last time I saw the BeadforLife beaders, on fire with their new future, they were at a community meeting, sitting around under an open-air shelter where we'd earlier danced. Director Torkin Wakefield was guiding the women to imagine and harness their new future—an often difficult thing, since they've had to learned to live in the present to survive.

Breathe deeply and envision your new businesses, Wakefield urged the beaders: "Visualize a peaceful future of health and sisterhood. Now visualize your children in school, hoards of customers coming to your new businesses. See yourself enjoying your streams of income. See your business thriving. See yourself happy and well."

I watched many of the beaders, their eyes closed, smiling widely. I imagined they must be reflecting on their new village, stores, markets, and customers. Suddenly, the women burst into laughter, cracking up so much their bodies shook. A few threw their heads back and slapped their knees. I can't wait to see what happens in their world. The beaders of BeadforLife are, for sure, a force to be reckoned with.

As is this new give-back movement rockin' our world.

Connecting

Please report back from your more connected world. I wish you the best of journeys and the ultimate service adventures, however they unfold for you. Report back what you discover and how it's transformed not just a bit of the world around us, but your own world as well.

I would love to hear your volunteering and service experiences, either abroad or from home. You can submit them at my website: www.susanskog.com

Resources

Here's a sampling of some of the general voluntourism websites, which provide a roundup of volunteer trips and links to the appropriate volunteer-vacation organizations. The International Volunteer Programs Association site (www.ivpa.org) also lists its member volunteer-travel organizations that have met its rigorous standards.

Other websites that can link you to voluntourism opportunities, domestic and international, are as follows:

www.idealist.org
www.voluntourism.com
www.volunteerabroad.com
www.gonomad.com
www.networkforgood.com
www.glimpsefoundation.org
www.transitionsabroad.com
www.volunteermatch.org
www.goabroad.com

www.studenttraveler.com

www.worldvolunteerweb.com

Volunteer-Vacation and Service Organizations

Here's a small but mighty sampling of some of the voluntourism, or service vacation, organizations, many of which are leaders in the industry. More detailed descriptions of their offerings are found in Part Three, categorized by the type of volunteering you can do, from improving global health to easing environmental degradation.

Most of these organizations' websites offer alumni stories, as well as their history, mission, accomplishments, and other valuable information.

Amazon Promise: www.amazonpromise.org

Amigos de las Américas: www.amigoslink.org

Amizade: www.amizade.org

Cross-Cultural Solutions: www.crossculturalsolutions.org

Earthwatch: www.earthwatch.org

Global Citizens Network: www.globalcitizens.org

Global Crossroad: www.globalcrossroad.com

Global Vision International: www.gviusa.com

Global Volunteer Network: www.volunteer.org.nz

Global Volunteers: www.globalvolunteers.org

Globe Aware: www.globeaware.org

Greenforce: www.greenforce.org

i-to-i.: www.i-to-i.com

Peacework: www.peacework.org

Projects Abroad: www.projects-abroad.org

Pro World Service Corps www.myproworld.org

Sierra Club: www.sierraclub.org

United Planet: www.unitedplanet.com

Village Volunteers: www.villagevolunteers.org

Volunteer Africa: www.volunteerafrica.org

Volunteer Kenya: www.volunteerkenya.org

Volunteer Visions. www.volunteervisions.org

Volunteers for Peace: www.vfp.org

Wilderness Volunteers: www.wildernessvolunteers.org

World Endeavors: www.worldendeavors.org

WorldTeach: www.worldteach.org

Also check out these sites as you look at your options:

Travelocity: Travelocity's Travel for Good Change Ambassadors Program aims to make it easier for travelers to experience volunteering around the world. It offers Change Ambassadors grants to subsidize volunteer vacations through Travel for Good's designated volunteer partners. www.travelocity.com

Fly for Good: Fly for Good helps you find volunteer opportunities and discounted airfares for international nonprofit travel. www.flyforgood.com

The following is a list of the humanitarian nonprofit and other organizations listed throughout the book. (If you ever want to monitor the track record and accountability of any nonprofit, go to websites like www.guidestar.com or www.charityguide.com.)

AARP: www.aarp.org

Abraham Path: www.abrahampath.org

Accion International: www.accion.org

Acumen Fund: www.acumenfund.org

AIDS Health Project: www.ucsf-ahp.org

Appropriate Infrastructure Development Group: www.aidg.org

Architecture for Humanity: www.architectureforhumanity.org

Armenia Tree Project: www.armeniatree.org

Ashoka: www.askoka.org

Asiana Education Development: www.asianaeducationdevel
opment.org

Backpack Club: www.thebackpackclub.org

BeadforLife: www.beadforlife.org

Bill and Melinda Gates Foundation: www.gatesfoundation.org

Building Blocks International: www.bblocks.org

Building Bridges Coalition: www.wevolunteer.net

Building with Books: www.buildingwithbooks.org

Career Gear: www.careergear.org

Case Foundation: www.casefoundation.org

Central Asia Institute: www.ikat.org

Citizen Schools: www.citizenschools.org

City Year: www.cityyear.org

Common Ground: www.commonground.org

Compassionate Listening: www.compassionatelistening.org

Cunningham Foundation: www.cunninghamfoundation.org

Dining for Women: www.diningforwomen.org

Doctors Without Borders: www.doctorswithoutborders.org

Dress for Success: www.dressforsuccess.org

Elton John AIDS Foundation: www.ejaf.org

Engineers Without Borders–USA: www.ewb-usa.org

Experience Corps: www.experiencecorps.org

FINCA International: www.villagebanking.org

Free the Children: www.freethechildren.com

Global Giving: www.globalgiving.org

Global Youth Connect: www.globalyouthconnect.org

Grameen Bank: www.grameen-info.org

Habitat for Humanity: www.habitat.org

Health Volunteers Overseas: www.hvousa.org

Heifer International: www.heifer.org

Homeboy Industries: www.homeboy-industries.org

Icouldbe: www.icouldbe.org

International Association of Physicians in AIDS Care: www.iapac.org

Keep a Child Alive: www.kcabeta.org

KickStart: www.kickstart.org

Kiva: www.kiva.org

Lawyers Without Borders: www.lwob.org

Malaria No More: www.malarianomore.org

MBAs Without Borders: www.mbaswithoutborders.org

Medical Teams International: www.medicalteams.org

Millennium Promise: www.millenniumpromise.org

Nonviolent Communication: www.nonviolentcommunication.com

Nothing but Nets: www.nothingbutnets.net

ONE: www.one.org

One World Classrooms: www.oneworldclassrooms.org

One World Youth Project: www.oneworldyouthproject.org

Opportunity International: www.opportunity.org

Oprah's Angel Network: www.oprah.com

Orphans Against AIDS: www.orphansagainstaids.org

Partners in Health: www.pih.org

PATH: www.path.org

Peace Corps: www.peacecorps.org

PeacePlayers International: www.peaceplayersintl.org

PeaceWorks Foundation: www.peaceworks.net

Pennies for Peace: www.penniesforpeace.org

Play for Peace: www.playforpeace.org

Points of Light: www.pointsoflight.org

Project C.U.R.E.: www.projectcure.org

Project Education Sudan: www.projecteducationsudan.org

ProLiteracy Worldwide: www.literacyvolunteers.org

Pump Aid: www.pumpaid.org

Room to Read: www.roomtoread.org

Roots and Shoots: www.rootsandshoots.org

Seeds of Peace: www.seedsofpeace.org

Share Our Strength: www.shareourstrength.org

Software Without Borders: www.softwarewithoutborders.com

Stayin' Alive: www.malarianomore.org/stayinalive

Stephen Lewis Foundation: www.stephenlewisfoundation.org

Tap Project: www.tapproject.org

Teach for America: www.teachforamerica.org

Teachers Without Borders: www.teacherswithoutborders.org

TreeGreetings: www.treegreetings.com

Trees for the Future: www.treesftf.org

Unitus: www.unitus.com

Veterinarians Without Borders: www.veterinarianswithout
borders.org

Voz: www.portlandvoz.org

Water 1st: www.water1st.org

Water Advocates: www.wateradvocates.org

Water for People: www.waterforpeople.org

William J. Clinton Foundation: www.clintonfoundation.org

Women for Women International: www.womenforwomen.org

World Neighbors: www.wn.org

Year Up: www.yearup.org

Index

About the Author

Trained as a journalist, Susan Skog has written about humanitarians and their projects for fifteen years. She is the author of five nonfiction books, including *Peace in Our Lifetime* and *Embracing Our Essence*, and her work has also appeared in many leading magazines and newspapers.

Skog is a former manager at Engineers Without Borders–USA. She has worked with and volunteered for BeadforLife, which supports Ugandan women, many of whom are HIV-positive refugees. A public speaker, Skog has presented at organizations and conferences around the country. She and her family live in Fort Collins, Colorado.